THINKERS OF OUR TIME

OAKESHOTT

THINKERS OF OUR TIME

OAKESHOTT

Robert Grant

The Claridge Press
London

All rights reserved. No part of this publication may be reproduced or transmitted in any form or by any means, including photocopying and recording, without the written permission of the copyright holder, application for which should be addressed to the publishers. Such written permission must also be obtained before any part of this publication is stored in a retrieval system of any nature.

First published in Great Britain 1990

by The Claridge Press
6 Linden Gardens
London W2 4ES
and Box 420
Lexington
Georgia 30648

Copyright © Robert Grant 1990

Typeset by
Fingerprint Graphics
London N1
and printed by
Short Run Press
Exeter, Devon

ISBN 1-870626-61-3 (Hardback)

ISBN 1-870626-66-4 (Paperback)

Grant, Robert: *Oakeshott*

1. Political Science

Contents

	Preface	7
	Textual References	8
	Introduction	9
1.	Life and Works	11
2.	The Background of Oakeshott's Thought	25
3.	The Modes (I): the Basic Theory	37
4.	Practice, Reason and Tradition	45
5.	The Modes (II): the Conversation Paradigm	65
6.	Agency, Association, and the State	71
7.	The Modes (III): History and Poetry	99
8.	Oakeshott and Contemporary Thought	111
	Appendix	119
	Further Reading	121
	Index	124

In Memoriam

Flint Schier (1958-1988)

Preface

This study was completed in October 1989. Had it appeared the following February as originally planned, it would have been the first single-handed book-length treatment of Oakeshott for almost a generation, and also, since Oakeshott has produced three new works in the interim, the only one to cover his entire output. In the event those honours have gone to Professor Paul Franco (see Further Reading). But there is still a need, which I hope the present work goes some way to meet, for a short introduction, addressed not to the academic political scientist, but to the ordinary interested reader or student. Accordingly, I have assumed no previous knowledge of Oakeshott and the Idealist tradition, and have tried to keep things as simple as possible. Given the nature of Idealism, however, that is rarely as simple as one would like, and the reader should not begrudge a little patience here and there (e.g. in Chapter 2).

For criticising my first draft (which I have also amended slightly in the light of subsequent Eastern European events), I am greatly indebted to John Gray, Sandra Kemp, Michael Lessnoff, Anthony O'Hear, Joseph Sobran, and the editor of this series, Roger Scruton. A number of people, notably Peregrine Worsthorne, but most of all Michael Oakeshott himself, have provided me with valuable biographical information.

I dedicate this book to the memory of my friend and colleague at Glasgow University, Flint Schier (1953-1988). Had I been able to consult him during its composition, it would not only have been better, but it would also have been completed in half the time.

Glasgow, August 1990

Textual References

The following are the editions or sources referred to. Most are unique. Where they are not, I have once or twice preferred, while giving the main reference, to quote Oakeshott's earlier version. Sometimes, where I thought it useful, I have given a double reference, e.g. R 248/A 75 (the first page in each case of 'The Moral Life in the Writings of Thomas Hobbes'). The appropriate letter is followed by the page number.

I have been lavish with references since only E, H and V have anything like an adequate index, while R, one of the most important, has no index at all.

A *Hobbes on Civil Association*, Berkeley 1975
C *On Human Conduct*, Oxford 1975
D *The Social and Political Doctrines of Contemporary Europe*,
    Cambridge 1939
E *Experience and its Modes*, Cambridge 1933 (also 1966, 1978,
    1985)
H *On History and Other Essays*, Oxford 1983
J1 *Cambridge Journal*, Vol. 1 (1947-8)
J4 *Cambridge Journal*, Vol. 4 (1950-1)
M 'The Masses in Representative Democracy', in A. Hunold, ed.,
    Freedom and Serfdom, Dordrecht 1961
P 'The Claims of Politics', in *Scrutiny*, Vol. 8 (1939-40)
R *Rationalism in Politics and Other Essays*, London 1962 (also
    1974)
V *The Voice of Liberal Learning*, New Haven, 1989

Introduction

Michael Oakeshott is probably the greatest living political philosopher in the Anglo-Saxon tradition. He is certainly the most original, the most cultivated, and the most wide-ranging. Nevertheless, though well-known in his own discipline, and to some extent also among historians, 'pure' philosophers, and academic lawyers, he has founded nothing so tangible as a school. No administration or political party has retained him as an adviser, or publicly identified itself with his ideas. Neither at home (the United Kingdom) nor abroad has he received any notable public honours. Unlike Professors Hayek, Friedman and Galbraith, and formerly Laski (to whose chair at the London School of Economics he succeeded in 1951), he has not become a global guru. As for the general public, even the general educated public, it has never heard of him.

There are a number of reasons for Oakeshott's low public profile. First, he is a modest, retiring man, with an instinctive aversion to the limelight. A trenchant critic of the post-war collectivist consensus, he has nevertheless shrunk from open polemics against it, and has claimed none of the credit for its recent demise. The spirit of controversy, indeed, is radically alien to his outlook.

Secondly, though there is much of the classical liberal in his make-up, Oakeshott is also a conservative. Ever since Mill first identified it with 'the stupider party', conservatism - the creed also of Aristotle, Hobbes, Hume, Burke, Hegel, T.S. Eliot and other notorious dunces - has been something of a bar to intellectual advancement. But Oakeshott's version, though broadly in tune with the tacit, unreflecting conservatism of the ordinary man, is also ill-calculated to appeal to official Conservatism, various though that may be. Too indifferent to establishment and hierarchy for the High Tory, it is also too sceptical for the moralist, too liberal for the populist, too principled for the mere pragmatist, and too divergent from whatever contradictory priorities (e.g. wealth-creation and moral restorationism) may be supposed fitfully to animate the current British and American administrations.

Finally, Oakeshott's is more a style of thinking than a set of articles or assumptions, still less (and unlike one of its major rivals, Marxism) a set of conclusions. Though for the most part clearly, forcefully, and even elegantly expressed, Oakeshott's thought cannot be reduced to a series of hard-edged, quasi-mathematical formulae. It is not a calculus, a method, or an ideology. It promises no short cuts to wisdom or right action. One of Oakeshott's central contentions, indeed, is that neither a man's thought, nor the social practices out of which it emerges, are properly susceptible of reduction. 'To know only the gist,' he has written, 'is to know nothing' (R 129).

It follows that, unlike Hobbes and Bentham, or most recently Rawls and Nozick, Oakeshott holds little appeal for the dialectician. Where there are neither axioms nor propositions, there can be neither refutation nor proof. Oakeshott's thought is less a self-conscious theoretic edifice than a slowly-unfolding imaginative world minutely responsive to the contours of the collective human experience it purports to chart. It is a world which, because it contains few dragons, is apt to prove a disappointment to the dragon-slayer. To understand it demands patience, a willingness to suspend judgment, and a certain basic sympathy with Oakeshott's implicit aims and procedures. Much in it, inevitably, is open to criticism. Yet properly understood, it has a gravity and a gaiety, a depth and a delightfulness, a complexity and a coherence, and even an underlying, consolatory idealism of its own.

1. Life and Works

The second of three brothers (all of whom survive), Michael Oakeshott was born in 1901, to parents of the unaffluent but educated and public-spirited middle class. His mother, a London vicar's daughter, trained as a nurse; during the First World War she was commandant of a small military hospital. She took a lifelong interest in charitable work, and first met Oakeshott's father in that connection. He, the son of a Newcastle postmaster, was from the age of 16 a civil servant in the Inland Revenue Department at Somerset House, where he rose to the rank of Principal. Entirely without personal ambition, he devoted his life to bookish pursuits and above all, with his wife, to their children's education.

The boys and their mother would sing hymns round the piano on Sunday evenings. Oakeshott père, however, was an agnostic. He was also a friend of George Bernard Shaw, and a Fabian. He never imposed his views on his family. Nevertheless, it might be suspected that the younger Oakeshott's hostility to collectivism generally, and his dismissive references to Shaw and the Fabians (e.g. R 23, 38; C 300), were in some way a reaction against his father's ideas. But to dispel any such notion, here is his own account, from a letter to the present writer:

> My father ... was as modest about his politics as he was about his agnosticism. We never talked politics at home; neither we nor my mother were interested. ...
> [He] was most conscientious in observing the convention that Civil Servants don't publicly take part in politics. He used to go to Fabian Society meetings; he wrote a Fabian Pamphlet on the Reform of the Poor Law. I don't think he ever took to the Webbs ... He always voted Liberal (we were never in a constituency which had a Labour candi-

date) and I think, generally speaking, his politics were those of a J.S. Mill Liberal, though he didn't have much time for Asquith and had the greatest contempt for Lloyd George. The truth is that his interests were always more literary than political ... He was never a 'party' man, any more than I am, and the only political issue I can think of where I knew where he stood was Votes for Women, but of course he would have nothing to do with the Pankhursts. ...

[I do not think] that 'politics' at the level of opinion was a very significant part of his life, and it is certainly not with me.

Oakeshott and his father also shared a deep affection for the 16th-century French essayist and sceptic, Montaigne, whom Oakeshott often cites with approval (R 200, 290; C 87, 242, 321; etc.). It was also in a book of his father's - *The Diversions of Purley*, by the eccentric Regency radical and philologist Horne Tooke - that Oakeshott, at about the age of 16, first perceived the germ of what later became one of his own central ideas, that thought is invariably the shadow or precipitate of practice.

The next major formative influence on Oakeshott was St George's, Harpenden, the co- educational school he attended from the age of 11, and in particular its founder and Headmaster, the Rev. Cecil Grant (d. 1946). To judge from an anthology of former pupils' reminiscences, both St George's and Grant himself were remarkable institutions. Grant was a classic and a theologian, deeply pious in an undogmatic way, an art-lover of Pre-Raphaelite persuasion, a socialist (though he hated Shaw), a passionate believer in co-education, and a friend and admirer of the educational reformer Maria Montessori (who twice visited the school). He would devote his sermons, not to Christian doctrine (in which he apparently took little interest), but to such things as Kant's Categorical Imperative. On walking tours he would instruct 15-year-olds in Hegel's metaphysics.

The school was indelibly stamped with Grant's personality. Some pupils resented this. Most, however, and among them Oakeshott, seem to have been very happy. He has described his schooldays in an extended 'Personal Retrospect' included in the volume mentioned above. This book is publicly unobtainable, but since Oakeshott's contribution echoes many of his best-known passages and preoccupations elsewhere, and is thus of considerable interest, I have provided some excerpts from it in an appendix below.

From 1919 Oakeshott read History at Gonville and Caius College, Cambridge, taking the History of Political Thought option in both parts of the Tripos. He also attended an 'Introduction to Philosophy' by the Idealist McTaggart. Thematic rather than historical, this course was Oakeshott's own formal introduction to the subject.

Oakeshott had long been interested in theology, and, as a graduate student in the 1920's, twice visited the universities of Marburg (where, incidentally, Heidegger was lecturing) and Tubingen in order to pursue it further. Already well-read in German literature, there Oakeshott read Hölderlin, Nietzsche and Burckhardt, and went tramping off with the Wandervögel. This was an informal student movement dedicated to nature-worship, camping out, and (according to D.H. Lawrence) 'free love'. Though very much of its time and place (Weimar Germany), it also embodied a traditional vein of German Romanticism, harmless enough and even valuable in itself, which the National Socialists were later to exploit. Its main legacy to Oakeshott, however, seems to have been his taste for solitude and the simple life (even in later life he has regularly wandered off on camping expeditions by himself). Typically of Oakeshott, however, this has been a taste by no means exclusive of its opposite.

After a brief spell as senior English master at Lytham St Anne's Grammar School, Oakeshott returned in 1927 to a Fellowship at his old College. He did a lot of teaching, especially in Modern History, and it was out of his lectures that his first book developed, *Experience and its Modes*. He was already reviewing works on philosophy and theology for the *Cambridge Review* and specialist journals, and produced his first independent essay, a pamphlet on 'Religion and the Moral Life', in this year. In both style and content, and like *Experience and its Modes*, it recalls the Oxford Idealist F.H. Bradley; its conclusions are Bradley's, to the effect that religion, rather than being the buttress or sanction of morality, is essentially its 'ideality' or 'completion' (*cf.* E 292, C 83).

Experience and its Modes appeared in 1933, when Oakeshott was 31. It received enthusiastic notices from R.G. Collingwood in the *Cambridge Review* and T.M. Knox in the *Oxford Magazine*, a respectful review in *Philosophy* (which remarked on the author's 'truly high capacity for literary art'), and some tart, not to say sniffy, remarks from L. Susan Stebbing in *Mind*. She found the section on Science 'peculiarly unsatisfying', and concluded by saying that 'those who have not been convinced by Bradley are not likely to be converted by Mr Oakeshott'.

History was to vindicate Miss Stebbing, at least in the short run. The first edition of *Experience and its Modes* took over thirty years to sell. The truth, however, was simply that the day of Idealism had passed, and that of Logical Positivism had dawned. Such are the vicissitudes of intellectual fashion, though, that *Experience and its Modes* has been reprinted three times since the 1960's.

Since his book had been admired by people he respected, Oakeshott seems not to have been greatly distressed by its fate. He has never aspired to join the philosophical establishment, and (he says) has communicated since then with only two 'official' philosophers, Gilbert Ryle and another Oxonian, the Hegelian G.R.G. Mure. If Oakeshott's thought is radically opposed to that of the Logical Positivists, and hence to that of the earlier Wittgenstein, it has something in common with the later Wittgenstein. Nevertheless, though Oakeshott and Wittgenstein were at Cambridge together for nearly twenty years, they never met.

Oakeshott has always pursued his wide intellectual interests in his own way and at his own pace. In the 1930's he developed an interest in Hobbes, and has since become one of the world's leading Hobbes scholars. He wrote on Hobbes and (damningly) on Bentham for F.R. Leavis's journal *Scrutiny*. But once again, though (urbanity of mind excepted) Leavis and he had much in common, by his own account Oakeshott never once set eyes on him. (Leavis - for better or worse, the most influential literary critic of the century - spent his whole life in Cambridge.)

It may be wondered how Oakeshott contrived to be so much out of the swim. Some of his critics (not for the first time) will point to his *A Guide to the Classics*, or, *How to Pick the Derby Winner* (with G.T. Griffith, 1936), and imply that, while Europe was coming to the boil, Oakeshott (Nero-like) was lounging with the toffs at Newmarket. The truth is more prosaic. Fired by his co-author and Caius colleague, Guy Griffith, a keen racing man, Oakeshott did indeed make a serious and enthusiastic study of the sport. But having once thrown light into that far from unimportant corner of national culture (one recalls T.S. Eliot's bracketing-together of Elgar, the Derby, and pickled beetroot as typically 'English'), Oakeshott moved on. (He has not, he says, been to a race-meeting since the Second World War.) Nevertheless, *A Guide to the Classics* is a key exhibit for those who would write him off as a 'Tory dandy'. For others it will merely confirm that there is little *terra incognita* on Oakeshott's map of the world.

The 'Thirties - Auden's 'low, dishonest decade' - were marked by strident demands among the intelligentsia for intellectual and political 'commitment'. Oakeshott's final contribution to *Scrutiny* appeared in 1939, in a symposium called 'The Claims of Politics'. Amid the clamour of his fellow-symposiasts, Oakeshott's piece is remarkable for its sublime, even breathtaking, aloofness. The muchtrumpeted 'claims of politics', he thought, were inconsiderable compared with the cultural and intellectual life it was the business of politics to protect. In itself, politics is 'vulgar', 'bogus', and 'callous', not merely because it attracts people of that stamp, but 'because of the false simplification of human life implied in even the best of its purposes' (P 148).

Oakeshott, of course, was by no means ignorant of world events, as his brilliant, and to this day indispensable, anthology of *The Social and Political Doctrines of Contemporary Europe* testifies. This (with Oakeshott's introduction and commentary) also came out in 1939, and was twice reprinted. The said doctrines, he wrote (totalitarianism being primarily in question), 'are striking mainly in virtue of their defects as doctrines and their remarkable success in subjugating whole communities.' He has some respect for political Catholicism, both on account of its intellectual coherence, and also because, though authoritarian, it is so 'without the capriciousness of the other authoritarian doctrines'. But for all its muddle and incoherence, it is Representative Democracy that Oakeshott finds the least unattractive. One of its 'central principles' (and also his own) is that 'the imposition of a universal plan of life on a society is at once stupid and immoral' (D xix, xxiii).

Oakeshott joined the Army immediately on the outbreak of war, and eventually commanded a squadron, attached to the Canadian Second Army in Holland, of the GHQ Liaison Regiment, alias 'Phantom'. ('Phantom' was a freelance, quasi-Signals, intelligence-gathering force.) The journalist Peregrine Worsthorne, who served under Oakeshott, has both spoken and written of his excellence as a commander: of his self-effacement, of the quiet efficiency of his administration, and of his mastery of everyday battlefield practicalities.

Military life, Oakeshott has said, always held a deep fascination for him, similar to that which it held for Alfred de Vigny (the author of *Servitude et Grandeur Militaires*). Yet, like Hobbes, Oakeshott is one of the most pacific of serious political thinkers. It is evident from his writings that, if the war made a deep impression on him, it was by no means an altogether romantic one. First, the war seems to have convinced him of a key article in his post-war reflections, the inadequacy of mere technical knowledge, such as he himself easily acquired: 'the intelligent civilian,' he has noted, 'always remained at a disadvantage beside the regular officer, the man educated in the feelings and emotions as well as the practices of his profession' (R 34n.). And secondly, it seems to have persuaded him that military organisation, being necessarily directed to a single overriding end, is the worst of all possible models for peacetime society, where the ends pursued are as various as those who pursue them (R 52, 56; C 272-4; V 116). This view contrasts sharply with that of those 1945 socialists who, impressed by the 'efficiency' of wartime collectivism (which, Oakeshott says, was actually 'exceedingly uneconomical'), proposed to 'win the peace' by the same methods (*cf.* J1 477). And not only does war create collectivism, but the reverse also holds: 'large-scale collectivism,' Oakeshott writes, 'is inherently warlike: the condition of things in which it is appropriate in the end makes its appearance.'

Not normally clubbable, Oakeshott seems to have enjoyed the raffish company he found in the Army. 'He loved social life,' Worsthorne has said, 'but always as the amused onlooker.' Among his junior officers was the Hon. Michael Astor, whose father, the 2nd Viscount Astor, was immensely rich, proprietor of the *Observer* newspaper, and a Tory grandee. On leave, Astor would take Oakeshott to Cliveden, the family's house on the Thames near Maidenhead, notorious in the 1930's as the meeting-place of the allegedly appeasement-minded 'Cliveden set'. Here Oakeshott once more mingled in a world very different from the one he had been accustomed to.

Oakeshott's critics on the left have been quick to pounce on his sole reference to this way of life, as though he were laying claim to it as his natural element. But Oakeshott is merely, in the admirable Victorian phrase, 'a scholar and a gentleman'. When he likens the ignorant modern politician to 'a foreigner or a man out of his social class ... bewildered by a tradition and a habit of behaviour of which he knows only the surface', and adds that 'a butler or an observant house-maid has the advantage of him' (R 31), it is not inconceivable that he himself may have experienced some such Prufrock-like embarrassment at Cliveden. For, as Scott Fitzgerald said, the very rich are 'different from us', and not merely because, as Hemingway quipped in reply, 'they have more money'.

Oakeshott returned to Cambridge after the war, and in 1946 published his edition of Hobbes's *Leviathan*, with its well-known Introduction (now reprinted separately in *Hobbes on Civil Association*). In 1947 he and a few colleagues started *The Cambridge Journal*, a lively intellectual review of remarkably high standard for a monthly (it ran until 1952). It was non-partisan, and for the most part not even political in content; the journal *Politics and Letters*, however, with which the late Raymond Williams was associated, hailed it on its appearance as 'patrician fare'.

Oakeshott soon became the *Cambridge Journal*'s star performer, and before long its General Editor. The earlier essays in his *Rationalism in Politics* appeared in it, as did 'The Universities' (reprinted, as I write, in *The Voice of Liberal Learning*), together with 'Scientific Politics', 'Contemporary British Politics', and 'Mr Carr's First Volume', which Oakeshott has not yet republished. Many will have wondered, like me, how, among his day-to-day editorial, teaching, and (copious) ordinary book-reviewing commitments, Oakeshott found time for such things, which are conceived on the very highest intellectual level, and written, moreover, with great pith and elegance. They may be interested to learn that the last-mentioned, a substantial review article on E.H. Carr's *The Bolshevik Revolution*, was composed in a single night.

After a brief period at Nuffield College, Oxford, Oakeshott, now 49, moved to the Chair of Political Science at the London School of Economics. In many ways, his predecessor being the socialist Harold Laski, his appointment was a symbolic end to the Attlee era (which nevertheless survived in intellectual life for almost thirty years more). Oakeshott's inaugural lecture, 'Political Education' (1951, R 111f.), though widely recognised as a distinguished utterance, generated on a more public scale the same kind of incomprehension, discomfiture, and in some cases near-outrage among the enlightened classes as his essay 'Rationalism in Politics' had already provoked.

I shall deal with these pieces later on. Suffice it to say here that they were bound to offend many if not most of his audience on each occasion. Oakeshott attacked, not socialism specifically, but the whole post-Enlightenment style of thought - 'rationalism' - to which in his view it belongs. The Rationalist believes essentially that there is only one kind of 'reason', that it is external to, and valid independently of, the activities to which it is applied, and that his possession of it gives him both the power and the authority to reorganise the world in accordance with its dictates. These dictates find articulation in an 'ideology': that is, in some comprehensive, self-legitimating, and (usually) pseudo-scientific programme of action. Rationalism, in short, is the 'planner's' mentality; while ideology is the 'plan', complete with justification.

Oakeshott's objection was not so much that 'planning' is a threat to freedom (though it is that), as that the whole Rationalist approach is misconceived. Because it is, and even makes a virtue of being, external to its objects, it can never acquire full knowledge of them. (Such knowledge is contained only in the unselfconscious traditions which have emerged from them and govern their constant evolution.) The Rationalist's 'plans' are bound in practice not only to fail, but also to destroy both future activity and its spring. The 'efficiency' of planning turns out to be a sham. So Rationalism is actually irrational.

No-one, and particularly not an intellectual, likes to be called a fool. For the most part Oakeshott's critics simply plunged deeper into the confusion between rationalism and genuine rationality from which he had been at pains to deliver them. In their view he had impugned, not the perversion of reason, but reason itself. He was guilty of irrationalism, even of mysticism. (Doubtless they did not know that he had already argued specifically against these heresies in 'Scientific Politics': see J1 349, 354-5 and *cf.* R 128n.) But ever since *Experience and its Modes*, his point had been that each activity generates its own, appropriate kind of rationality. The outcry against him was essentially that of the child deprived of his comforter, or told that he cannot have the moon.

Whatever hostility Oakeshott may initially have faced, he seems to have been a success at LSE. His lectures were packed with students from all disciplines. Non-specialists were especially impressed by the clarity and eloquence with which he laid bare the subtleties of Hobbes and Hegel, Mill and Green. Unusually for a good conversationalist, Oakeshott invariably read from a fully written-out script. He has said that he does not trust himself to speak from notes or think on his feet.

During the 'fifties Oakeshott produced a classic defence of the so-called 'autonomy of history' ('The Activity of Being an Historian'); a defence of conservatism, remarkable for dispensing with just about everything (bar the rule of law) that conservatives have ever thought important ('On Being Conservative'); and 'The Voice of Poetry in the Conversation of Mankind', a long essay on aesthetics, which not only introduces Oakeshott's novel and important conception of the human world as 'conversation', but also makes substantial claims for what is in essence the autonomy of the aesthetic.

All of these, together with his longer *Cambridge Journal* pieces, a new study of Hobbes, and an essay on 'The Study of Politics in a University', were finally incorporated in *Rationalism in Politics and Other Essays* (1962). Oakeshott's corpus is often (though I think wrongly) regarded as somewhat slender. It is true that he has never been in a hurry to publish, and, academically speaking, belongs to a far more leisurely (and cultivated) age than the present. Few readers of these ten essays, nevertheless, will deny that Oakeshott's reticence has paid off. Whether or not one agrees with them, it must be admitted that they contain enough material for several books, and more real, deeply-pondered thought than hundreds upon hundreds of quotidian productions. The reader whose interest has been seriously engaged is likely to find that he can, over the years, return to these essays again and again with renewed pleasure and surprise.

Rationalism in Politics offers little advice to the practising politician, except (the most valuable of all) that he should give up his nostrums and trust instead to taste, experience, and the power of institutions themselves to suggest the directions they should take. Probably no-one (except in Communist countries) will ever go armed with it to the barricades. But for all that (which is in any case a virtue) it is surely a classic.

Oakeshott retired in 1968, before the French student disorders of that year spread to LSE. The department he left behind had acquired a decidedly Oakeshottian cast, a fact which caused resentment amongst traditionally radical LSE staff in other departments, and later led to some unseemly public squabbles. In these Oakeshott himself took no part. He was in any case busy on his third book, *On*

Human Conduct (1975). He also, between 1967 and 1975, wrote the three longest of the educational essays now republished in *The Voice of Liberal Learning*.

On Human Conduct is the most inspissated of Oakeshott's longer works, more so even than *Experience and its Modes*. In some ways it is a completely new departure, being the first book of his that can reasonably be expected to baffle, or even repel, the casual reader. (For that reason it is not a good one for the would-be student of Oakeshott to start with; *Rationalism in Politics* is far and away the best in that respect.) *On Human Conduct* depends for its intelligibility on the reader's having taken some trouble to master its novel terminology. The book consists of three long, interconnected essays. In the first, Oakeshott distinguishes physical 'processes' from human (i.e. intelligent) 'practices' or 'procedures', and divides action itself into two components, 'self-disclosure' (the advertisement of wants), and 'self-enactment' (the realization of character); in the second, he distinguishes 'civil association' (conceived in terms of law) from 'enterprise association' (conceived in terms of purpose); in the third, he traces two correlative conceptions of the modern European state, identifying the 'civil' state with post-Renaissance 'individuality', and the 'enterprise' state (essentially the 'rationalist' state) with the 'anti-individual' or 'mass' man.

'The themes explored here,' Oakeshott writes, 'have been with me almost as long as I can remember.' This is true enough. But one might just add that much in the first section of *On Human Conduct* was developed from ideas first fielded in 'The Voice of Poetry' and Oakeshott's educational writings; much in the third from an essay (first published in German in 1957, and in English in 1961) called 'The Masses in Representative Democracy'; and much in the second which pertains to the 'rule of law' from 'On Being Conservative' and 'The Political Economy of Freedom' (the latter, also in *Rationalism in Politics*, is in part a defence of Chicago economics, which Oakeshott discovered a quarter of a century before Sir Keith Joseph).

Also in 1975 Oakeshott added a codicil to *On Human Conduct* called 'The Vocabulary of a Modern European State' (in the journal *Political Studies*, Vol. 23), and collected his various pieces on Hobbes (bar the early *Scrutiny* essay) in *Hobbes on Civil Association*.

His next wholly new book, *On History and Other Essays*, appeared in 1983. It consists of three thematically unrelated pieces: the title essay is the culmination of a lifetime's reflection on the historian's task; the second is an essay on the rule of law, an attempt (roughly speaking) to codify all Oakeshott's previous observations on the subject; while the third is an extended, and brilliantly imaginative, fable showing how authority in the 'enterprise state' must always be compromised by its engagement to do more for its subjects than merely rule them. It is in marked contrast with its companion pieces, which (like *On Human Conduct*) are tough going.

That, then, is the main Oakeshott canon. There is no reason to suppose it complete, for despite his great age Oakeshott continues to flourish in astonishing vigour of body and mind. Though an enthusiastic, unrepentant cigarette-smoker (see his sly note at C 170), and far from averse to a decent bottle of wine, he has always lived simply; his pied-à-terre during his LSE days lacked even a refrigerator. Staunch in his defence of civilisation and the subtle historic artifice by which it has been built up, he nevertheless has in him a great deal of the youthful, even innocent, bohemian and romantic. The simplest things have made him happy: a loaf warm from the baker's, a sunny morning, or (notoriously) a pretty face.

He now lives back in rural Dorset, amid an unpicturesque huddle of tiny, spartan, quarrymen's cottages. His own is heated by an open fire, furnished with a few odd sticks, and packed from floor to ceiling with books, in cases he has knocked together out of old floorboards. For decoration he has a few prints, and some paintings by his second wife (his first died in the 'fifties), whom he ferries daily, in his battered old sports car, to and from her studio in the nearest town. He still leads an active social life, making long train journeys to spend weekends with friends and former pupils. In his fisherman's cap, old mackintosh and balding Hush Puppies, no-one seems less the 'Tory dandy' than the great conservative philosopher of our time. It is only in his endearing warmth and civility, his conversability, his generosity of mind, that one catches a whiff of aristocracy; or rather, of that aristocratic spirit, shorn of all brutality, stiffness and arrogance, which the Renaissance humanists handed down to us in the form of liberal education, and which in truth, as Oakeshott would be the last to deny, is still to be found anywhere in society, from prince to pauper, that a tradition of moral education survives.

2. The Background of Oakeshott's Thought

Oakeshott's philosophical foundations are unusually explicit; his first book, indeed, is a work of systematic metaphysics in the Idealist manner. It is curious, but true, that although Oakeshott's politics turn largely upon a critique of 'rationalism' in his own, extended sense of that term, his metaphysics, which underpin them, have, like most Idealist thinking, a certain affiliation with rationalism in its strict or original sense.

Rationalism proper contends that the universe is knowable only to, or through, reason. Reason describes how things must be, experience merely how they appear to be. This disjunction between 'appearance' and 'reality' is central to rationalism as exemplified (say) by Plato, Descartes, Spinoza and Leibniz. It is not, however, peculiar to rationalism, being found also in religion, natural science, and much modern social thought (e.g. Marx and Freud). All of these, rationalism included, are what one might call 'strong' versions of realism. They allege, not merely (what realism in general alleges) that things exist independently of our experience, but also that our experience of them is significantly different from the way they are. Behind the empirical or phenomenal world - that is, the world as it presents itself in experience or consciousness - there lies some other, more or less invisible 'reality' or 'real world' (e.g. God, matter, the physicist's forces and particles, economic forces, the unconscious, etc.).

For Idealism, however (which is often thus capitalised to distinguish it from moral or political idealism), 'reality' is not distinct from experience, but identical with it. This does not mean that things are exactly as they seem to immediate experience (yours or mine), for obviously individual perspectives differ, and no one perspective can encompass ultimate reality, which is simply   experience as a whole. What it does mean is that appearances or 'seemings' are a real fact of life, to be taken account of accordingly, and not to be dismissed as illusory or superfluous. Further, it means that there is nothing 'outside' experience, nothing 'transcendent', no permanent 'hidden reality'. Experience therefore is self-authenticating; it cannot be guaranteed by anything more fundamental, because nothing more fundamental exists. To be real is simply to be 'in' experience, and every experience is an 'idea' (whence the name Idealism), i.e. a part or content of consciousness. Consciousness, moreover, cannot finally be distinguished from its contents, since it is always consciousness of something.

If experience is central to Idealism, so it is also to empiricism, rationalism's traditional opposite. Empiricism holds that experience, rather than reason, is the source and test of all genuine knowledge. It tends also to regard sense as the typical form of experience, and experience as a window on reality rather than reality itself. Idealism, however, abolishes all such distinctions. For Idealism, a deliverance of reason is as real as any sensory impression. Conversely, even sensory experience bears the marks of thought, which is reason *in posse*.

For example, my so-called 'sensation' of a tree is not actually distinct from the judgment (*sc*. thought) that 'this is a tree'. (If I do not see it as a tree, but merely, say, as a green patch, then, whatever anyone else sees, what I am seeing is not 'a tree' but 'a green patch'.) Thoughts even of this rudimentary kind are intrinsically subject to the objective laws of thought, *viz*. reason and logic, and are hence, if only in a limited way, rational. (For example, if this is a tree, it cannot be something else, i.e. not a tree.)

In essence, Idealism fuses rationalism with empiricism. The aim is to make reason less abstract, by giving it something concrete to work on, and to show at the same time that experience is intrinsically reasonable. If anything, though, Idealism leans towards the rationalist pole. Many if not most Idealists are notorious logic-choppers, and work at dauntingly high levels of abstraction. Reality is simply the ordered sum of appearances, i.e. whatever remains or subsists once all discontinuities have been ironed out, all partial perspectives reconciled, and all ambiguities resolved. Usually reality is conceived, as it is by Oakeshott in *Experience and its Modes*, as some sort of unitary Absolute or Whole. But Idealism's critics could and did say that this Absolute is purely notional, being as remote in practice from anybody's possible experience as any 'transcendent' so-called reality.

If they are right, then Idealism, at least of the so-called Absolute or Hegelian brand just characterised, is no more than a reformed rationalism. What still needs to be explained, and not by reference to some transcendent reality or quasi-transcendent Absolute, but in its own, local terms, is the everyday, intermediate world of experience. As we shall see, some such suspicion, while there from the start, seems increasingly to have come to the fore in Oakeshott's thinking, and to be not wholly unconnected with his rejection of socio-political Rationalism. He has not, however, ceased to be an Idealist; he has merely jettisoned the Absolute.

It is with Absolute Idealism, however, that we must begin our account of Oakeshott's intellectual background. Mind-based or experience-based philosophies such as Idealism (and also empiricism) are particularly liable to collapse into futile subjectivism. We have seen one escape from it, the contention that experience is intrinsically rational and hence 'objective'. The author of it, Hegel (1770-1831), also provides another. According to him, subject and object (the self and its world) exist, but only as aspects or precipitates of an undifferentiated experience prior to them both, that of pure 'Being' (an idea revived by Heidegger in our own century). 'Being' is objective simply in the sense of its being a brute fact, an irreducible given. I may and do participate in it without having first to experience myself as 'me', or it as in any way 'mine'. Hegel, the most thoroughgoing of the Idealists, here contrasts with Descartes (1596-1650), for whom the primary, irreducible fact was subjectivity (in the shape of the conviction that, whatever else may or may not exist, I certainly do).

Hegel's 'Being' is prior both genetically and ontologically: it is the unreflective infantile 'unity' (as Hegel calls it) of self and world from which each of us is launched into self-consciousness; and it is also, recaptured at a more complex level, the Absolute itself. The Absolute (also called the Idea) is, as we have already seen, the ultimate reality of things as disclosed to reason and consciousness at the end of their labours; a self-conscious Whole or all-inclusive Mind into which individual minds or subjects (and with them all their objects) have finally, and knowingly, been reabsorbed. This Whole is actually a single, self-subsistent individual; it is more or less the pantheistic *Deus sive natura* (God or Nature) of Spinoza (1632-77). Individuals in the usual sense, though real enough, are merely its parts or aspects; Spinoza calls them 'modes' or 'modifications' of his One Substance.

Aspiring to account for everything, Hegel rejects nothing as irrelevant. Thus appearances are not strictly speaking false. Since reality is identical with everything that exists, and appearances unquestionably exist, they must belong to reality, be continuous with it, be made (as they cannot be for the rationalist) of the same basic stuff. And since reality, in Hegel's view, can be fully laid bare by its own all-pervading principle of reason, it too, in the end, is 'appearance': not an appearance of something else (for there is nothing else) but simply appearance *tout court*. What rationalists reject as illusion is always, for Hegel, partial truth.

For Idealists generally 'truth' is not a property of sentences or propositions, but reality itself, the whole or the Absolute. Even if propositions could somehow refer to or capture reality, they would still be distinct from it, and hence partial. Truth is ultimately not semantic but ontological. Rightly or wrongly, Idealism is at odds with Logical Positivism, logical atomism, and scientific realism generally in regarding as meaningless - at least, in the final analysis - any concept of an 'external world' to which propositions might 'refer'. (This, of course, may be merely a matter of nomenclature. If 'truth' were taken to mean not 'reality', but only 'whatever corresponds to reality', a proposition could be 'true' without being fully 'real'.)

Hegel conceived of thought as progressing by stages or 'moments' to its final completion or self-realization in the Idea (the point at which it grasps its true identity with the Whole). Every successive such 'moment', therefore, though defective, will contain a greater measure of 'truth' than its predecessor. It will make sense, achieve a provisional coherence, until reason, exposing its inchoateness, forces it to ascend to the next platform of understanding.

For Hegel these provisional thought-worlds form a genetic or evolutionary hierarchy (as they clearly do in what Hegel himself takes to be their most typical instance, the stages through which the individual consciousness passes in its development from infancy to maturity). They differ in degree rather than in kind. Here Hegel diverges somewhat from his successors Bradley (1846-1924) and Collingwood (1889-1943).

Bradley's phenomenology (i.e. his account of consciousness and appearance) owes much to Hegel. Beginning from Feeling or Immediate Experience (Hegel's 'unity'), experience passes through two 'relational' stages. In the first, things are seen as intrinsically separate, being related to each other only 'externally'; in the second, relations are 'internal', in that each thing is actually defined, or constituted, by its relations to other things. Everything is organically connected with everything else. From there it is but a short step to the Absolute, in which relations are transcended, and everything is ultimately one thing.

I have spelt out Bradley's phenomenology because it lies behind Oakeshott's in *Experience and its Modes*. But Bradley also conceives of other spheres of experience distinguished less by structure than by content. These are not hierarchically related, but are independent of each other. In *Appearance and Reality* he calls them 'modes' (the Spinozan term that Oakeshott was also to adopt), and in *Essays on Truth and Reality* 'worlds'. They include 'the sensory sphere', 'the inner realm of ideas', 'the worlds of duty and religious truth', 'hope, desire and dream', 'the various worlds of politics, commerce, invention, trade and manufacture', 'the intellectual province of truth and science, and, more or less apart from this, the whole realm of the higher imagination'.

Bradley gave no common, systematic account of these 'worlds'. Collingwood, however, did so in his *Speculum Mentis* (1924). Influenced by the Italian Idealist Croce, Collingwood divided knowledge into the 'provinces' of Art, Religion, Science, History and Philosophy. Unlike Bradley, however, he also identified them as successive Hegelian 'moments'. Art is the primitive stage, in which imagination and fact are indistinguishable; Religion asserts the imaginary as fact; Science asserts abstract fact, only to be superseded by History or concrete fact, of which, like all else, it is ineluctably part. Philosophy is mind's knowledge of itself (and thus of the Absolute) but since mind can only know itself through the various worlds it has created, and since the Absolute exists nowhere else but in those worlds taken as a whole, Philosophy, rather than actually supplanting them, stands to them more in the relation of critic or cartographer.

As Collingwood explicitly says, the 'modes' for him cannot be truly autonomous, as they can be for Bradley, and as Oakeshott subsequently insists they must be. For the whole point of Oakeshott's attack on Rationalism (in his sense) is that the 'reason' (that is, the methods, presuppositions and conclusions) appropriate to any one mode of experience cannot, without irrelevance, be applied to any other. (A view which, oddly enough, Collingwood seems to share.)

Oakeshott and Collingwood nevertheless agree on much. (It is curious that Oakeshott claims not to have read *Speculum Mentis* until after he had completed *Experience and its Modes*, for the disagreements, like the agreements, are almost explicit: see, e.g. E 72, 84.) One or two further resemblances may be noted. The first is their common Idealist distrust of 'abstraction', by which is meant the propensity (in Collingwood's words) 'to consider separately things that are inseparable'. The second is illustrated by Collingwood's important distinction between the 'implicit' and the 'unconscious'. For both Oakeshott and Collingwood (as later for Sartre) the 'unconscious' is mere mumbo-jumbo, a relic of the discredited notion of transcendence. Whatever we are unaware of in experience, but which is nevertheless significant in that we might wish to be made aware of it, cannot be 'unconscious'. It is merely implicit (or, as Freud would say, 'preconscious'), since whatever is not in principle accessible to consciousness cannot exist for us.

Of course, the 'implicit' need not achieve its explicitness in theoretical or propositional terms. It may achieve perfectly adequate recognition in use or practice, which, though equally 'abstract' in the Idealist sense of being literally abstracted from the Whole to which it belongs, belongs to consciousness no less than propositional discourse does. Both Oakeshott and Collingwood stress the limitations of pure thought. In the end, a man's business is to live, and if philosophy can help him to do so more fully, it will, perhaps in spite of itself, have earned its keep. And even Bradley concurs in this distrust of intellectualism: 'our principles may be true,' he wrote in his *Principles of Logic,* 'but they are not reality.' Thought, to be real, must be more than an 'unearthly ballet of bloodless categories' (*cf.* Oakeshott's 'ghostly ballet of bloodless postulates', C 28). We have met with this criticism of Idealism's rationalist tendencies before, of course, but it is the more striking for being issued from within the very citadel of the faith.

It should be sufficiently obvious by now that, and how, a critical or negative politics can be derived from Idealist metaphysics. Idealism's respect for the concrete, the given, the historically-evolved, together with its distrust of abstraction and transcendence, align it generally speaking with the kind of sceptical conservatism disposed as far as possible to leave well, or even ill, alone. But it is certainly compatible also with liberalism, particularly where the prevailing political tradition is liberal. Only in its anti-individualism, its social and metaphysical holism, and (in some of its versions) its intimations of 'progress' towards some final redemptive consummation - though 'progress' of course is also an important strand in liberalism - does Idealism throw more ambiguous, or (some might claim) sinister, political shadows. The (so to speak) 'positive' politics of both Bradley and Hegel differ considerably from

Oakeshott's. Both are far more 'statist' than he. For them the State (at least ideally) is the moral will of Society made articulate: 'the self-conscious ethical substance' (Hegel); 'the real identity of might and right' (Bradley); even 'the march of God in the world' (Hegel again).

Oakeshott will have none of this. For him the State has value almost exclusively as the source and focus of law. He never exalts it as the voice of morality, a unitary 'community', or some kind of supra-individual Person, and never as (what in the last resort, such as war, it always is) undiluted, all-embracing power. In this (at least up to a point) he resembles his early teacher McTaggart, for whom the Absolute was not a single thing or Self, but (like the Stoics' Cosmopolis or Kant's 'Kingdom on Ends') a community of finite, autonomous selves. The State, says McTaggart, has no intrinsic value, and as to 'worshipping' it, 'it would be as reasonable to worship a sewage-pipe, which also possesses considerable value as a means.'

It seems doubtful whether, 'statist' though they were in many respects, Hegel and Bradley really denied Kant's Second Categorical Imperative, which requires that the individual should be treated 'never as a means only, but always also as an end in himself'. Certainly they believed, as Oakeshott does not, that the State is a microcosm of the Absolute, and, like it, literally and self-consciously an organism. But in an organism (at least according to Kant's definition) 'every part is reciprocally both means and end'. In political terms this would mean that the individual (or 'part') retains his status as an end. In other words, the State, if it really is an organism, must exist for the individual as much as the individual exists for the State. And even for Hegel and Bradley, the ideal or 'good' State exists nowhere but in, or by virtue of, the free, 'real', or 'rational' will of individuals (i.e. in what Rousseau - admired by both Kant and Hegel - would have called their General Will.)

Oakeshott, at least in his early work, may be called a collectivist in metaphysics. But in politics he remains something of a Kantian individualist. From the standpoint of the Absolute, doubtless, the individual lacks independent reality. But politics is not and cannot be the Absolute. It is no more and no less real than anything else that falls short of the whole. For Oakeshott politics belongs to the 'mode' of Practice, and one of the latter's essential presuppositions, without which life cannot be carried on, is 'the integrity and separateness of the self' (see E 271, where Oakeshott calls Hebbel, Kant, and D.H. Lawrence to his support).

There is in Kant a residual Cartesianism, which Oakeshott inherits via the neo-Kantians of the late 19th century, in particular Dilthey (1833-1911). Descartes' dualism of mind and matter, which Idealism laboured to abolish, persists in Kant to the extent that selves qua subjects must be transcendental. This is partly because the observing self by definition cannot, so to speak, catch itself in the act of consciousness. But more importantly, if selves belonged entirely to the empirical world of 'nature', they would be governed by its laws of cause and effect, and hence would not be 'free', something which, if morality is to have any meaning, it must be of their essence to be. (Kant did not explain how a transcendental self can 'act' on, or in, an empirical world; nor why the empirical world should be so constructed as to exclude subjectivity; nor - which is much the same thing - why subjectivity must necessarily be transcendental. For in ordinary life we generally have no difficulty in recognising each other, and not merely ourselves, as subjects.)

Dilthey divided knowledge into the *Naturwissenschaften* (natural sciences) and the *Geisteswissenschaften* (sciences of mind, or 'human' sciences), a dichotomy echoed in Oakeshott's later thought. For Dilthey the natural-scientific world is an abstraction, being the empirical world as subsumed under highly general categories and causal laws. Its 'hidden reality' (Dilthey's expression) is not directly accessible. Knowledge of it is therefore necessarily hypothetical.

The 'human' world, however, which corresponds to Kant's 'realm of freedom', is directly given in experience. (Dilthey thus virtually reverses Kant's classification: subjects are empirical, while 'nature' is more or less transcendental.) We know it first and foremost because we actually live it. It is a world of will, intention, and inter-subjective purpose. Any formal understanding of it, therefore, must depend precisely on our not ignoring or 'bracketing out' its essential intentionality. To do that would reduce it to a natural-scientific object. Rather, we must approach it in the spirit of empathy or *Verstehen*, that is, by taking, so far as we can, the events or utterances of which it consists in the sense 'meant' by the agents concerned.

All this is somewhat in the spirit of the mid-Victorian Idealist John Grote, whom Oakeshott has lately cited as worthy of the conservative's attention (*Spectator*, 9th July, 1988; *cf.* R 162n.). Grote stressed the essential 'knowableness' or 'adaptedness to reason' of things. This, of course, follows from the anti-realist point that so-called 'things' are not independent of us, but are none other than our own experience. As a result we can feel 'at home in the Universe'. The latter phrase was taken up by William James, whose pragmatism, however, unlike Oakeshott's, had both an irrationalist and a utilitarian, consequentialist tinge (see Oakeshott's criticisms of 'official' pragmatism: E 264f., 318; R 81, 100.)

Oakeshott is inclined to play down the importance of intention in the historian's understanding of things (see Chapter 7 below). Nevertheless, Dilthey's distinction lies behind his division of phenomena generally into (natural-scientific) 'processes' and (human or intelligent) 'procedures'. And Dilthey's *geistige Welt* (nowadays usually called, following Husserl, the *Lebenswelt*, or 'life-world') is explicitly invoked in Oakeshott's educational thinking: V 23, 45, 65).

As we shall see later, Oakeshott has important affinities with a number of contemporary thinkers. But so he does with many from his formative period, as they in turn do with the Romantics and Idealists of the nineteenth century and earlier. Like Ruskin, Carlyle, and particularly Burke (to whom he has often been compared) Oakeshott is a traditionalist, anti-mechanist and anti-rationalist. Yet his traditionalism has never taken a nostalgic or purely reactionary turn. Like Grote and Lotze, he is more than happy to endorse both mechanism and science in their proper spheres. And for all his superficial resemblance to (say) Bergson, he is (as already noted) anything but an irrationalist. Irrationalism, indeed, is for Oakeshott merely 'rationalism' in disguise (see, e.g., his comments on the Nazis, R 32, J1 351, and elsewhere). He is resolutely opposed to transcendental explanations, because the transcendental is not the premise or 'cause' of experience, but rather something to which, under certain conditions, experience seems inconclusively to point. In all these respects Oakeshott's debt to the Hegelian tradition would be clear enough even if he had not explicitly acknowledged it (E 6).

No more than Dilthey is Oakeshott really a Cartesian; whereas for Descartes the self was both private and absolute, for Oakeshott it is simply an inescapable feature of everyday experience, and, as such, to be respected and cultivated for what it is worth. For all his superficial dualism, Oakeshott belongs to a strongly anti-Cartesian tradition represented in his youth by (among others) Whitehead and later by Heidegger, Ryle and Wittgenstein. His thinking throughout has been humanistic and 'anti-essentialist', to the effect that (as Burke also believed) human beings for all practical purposes are what they take themselves to be (V 64). For this reason Oakeshott, though even friendlier to political freedom than Burke, is no less hostile than Burke was to the supposed 'natural rights' in which liberals often ground it (R 120, 135). 'Rights', like so-called 'human nature', are in fact not 'natural' at all, but an historic human artefact. Similarly, for Oakeshott, as for Hobbes, the 'right' of government must be artificial, even though it stems (as it did for Hume) from tradition or tacit convention rather than from any supposititious 'contract'.

Why, finally, if some human beings 'take themselves' to be 'essentially' souls, or animals, or automata, should we not accept their view of the matter? The answer would seem to be that qua human beings they can never act on any such basis, even if it should be as 'correct' as the view (not less an impediment to action) that they are partial manifestations of the Absolute. 'Abstract' though it is, practice would give them the lie. So the question arises whether after all practice is not the 'real' absolute, and thus the origin of the very thinking which condemns it to relativity.

3. The Modes (I): the Basic Theory

For anyone wishing to understand Oakeshott in depth *Experience and its Modes* is of cardinal importance. This precocious treatise contains the seeds not only of his politics, but also of his aesthetics, his reflections on historiography, his educational ideas, and of his later conception of the world as a continuous, pluralistic 'conversation'. By the first of many paradoxes endemic to Idealist thought, Oakeshott's pluralism emerges naturally out of his monism, and ends by almost supplanting it. The logic of this process, though nowhere fully explicit, seems to run something like this: unlike rationalism, Idealism allows that appearances, simply in virtue of existing, belong to the same order of reality as the Whole. They differ only in point of their inferior completeness, that is, of their relative 'abstraction', in Collingwood's sense (see previous chapter). But if appearance generally is part of the Whole, and to that extent 'real', the same must be true of the separate items of which it 'appears' to consist.

Further, if the parts in the end can be as real as the Whole, why could they not be yet more real than it? Might not the Whole, rather than the parts, be the abstraction, that is, a mere theoretical unity abstracted from the multifarious things, persons, studies, discourses, and practices - the *Lebenswelt*, in short - of which everyday experience consists? Indeed, is not the latter sense of the word 'abstraction' the normal one (and one notably exemplified by Rationalism, in Oakeshott's use of the term)? All that holds us back ultimately from a totally disintegrated, atomistic view of experience is our conviction that all this variety must still constitute a 'world', since we continue unreflectively so to describe it.

The aim of *Experience and its Modes* is nothing less than that of explaining everything (or at least of providing a basis from which everything can be explained). There is no space here to unravel all the paradoxes and contradictions into which Oakeshott's master-conception runs itself. But that master-conception needs at least to be stated if the book's detailed discussions of History, Science and Practice are to be understood.

The fundamental stuff of experience goes by the same name, Experience. Like Spinoza's 'God', it is the Whole; it is not, however, a static, quasi-material 'substance' but an evolutionary 'flow'. But unlike Bergson's aimless universal flux it is accessible to consciousness, and hence rational. To all intents and purposes it is dynamic Reason, and so far identical with Hegel's Absolute.

As in Hegel, however, it is not immediately perceptible in its full or developed character. In that character it is perceptible only to philosophy, which is notionally identical with it (for the Idealist conception of truth which leads to this unlikely-seeming conclusion, see Chapter 2 above). Experience discloses itself to humanity at large (as to the off-duty philosopher) only through a number of inevitable, relatively stable 'arrests' or backwaters in its current, the so-called 'modes' of experience (E 70-4, etc.).

As we have seen earlier, the term 'mode' (though not the thing itself) is originally scholastic and Spinozan. But Oakeshott inherits his 'modes' more directly from Bradley and Collingwood. As in Bradley, the number of possible modes is infinite, but Oakeshott chooses for analysis the three already mentioned, History, Science and Practice. A mode is essentially a particular, consistent way of seeing or conceiving the world, or the world as so seen; the product, roughly speaking, of a settled direction of attention. History sees the world under the aspect of the past; Science under that of quantity and regularity; and Practice under that of desire and value. Under Practice, which did not feature at all in Collingwood's scheme, Oakeshott includes both Art and Religion, which for Collingwood were distinct 'provinces'. (Oakeshott later made the aesthetic into a mode in its own right.)

Unlike Collingwood's, Oakeshott's modes are autonomous and (in virtue of their common abstraction as compared with Experience as a whole) equal in status. That is, they differ in kind rather than in degree. (Oakeshott occasionally asserts that they also represent different degrees of abstraction - see, e.g. E 84, 324 - but, as T.M. Knox pointed out, this is impossible if they are to remain equal.)

Every idea must belong to a mode; in other words, nothing can be apprehended except under some category or other. (Bradley noted in *Essays on Truth and Reality* that there are no 'floating' - that is, categorically homeless or indeterminate - ideas: *cf.* E 333-4, R 222.) And since an idea (or in everyday parlance, a 'thing') acquires its identity solely from its modal context (that is, from the other things in the same mode to all of which it is necessarily related), it follows that 'an idea cannot serve two worlds' (E 327). The scientist's H_2O and everyday 'water' are not variants or different aspects of a single substance, but two entirely different, abstract 'things' (*cf.* R 222). In Oakeshott's later writings, it should be said, this rigorous view proves almost impossible to sustain. For instance, an action (which is an 'idea' in the relevant sense) 'may be governed by different practices' (*sc.* modes, C 56); an 'object of use' may be 'contemplated' rather than used (R 149); and 'a word or a verbal construction' (e.g. 'The French Revolution') 'may have a home in more than one universe of discourse' (R 226). (If these are examples of mere homonymy, Oakeshott's local point in each case is lost.)

Be that as it may, in *Experience and its Modes* the modes, like Leibniz's 'windowless monads', are *sui generis* and mutually opaque. In consequence none of them has authority over any other. Modal 'truths' are determined solely by criteria internal to the mode concerned, and hold good nowhere else (E 77, 308, 310, etc.).

There is, of course, only one concrete, absolute truth, and that is Experience. Curiously, even philosophy, which (being itself Experience) is not a mode, has no authority - at least, no effective authority - to determine or intervene in a mode's internal affairs. Philosophy's business, says Oakeshott, is to root out and utterly destroy abstractions, and the modes are incurably abstract. Yet for that very reason philosophy cannot abolish them. Faced with humanity's obstinate propensity to think and act in modal terms, all it can do from its standpoint in the Absolute is emphasise the modes' relativity.

Roughly speaking, this office is equivalent to that of the Hobbesian sovereign in politics. For philosophy is the only thinking with sufficient authority to restrain the modes' intrinsic propensity to invade one another, in other words to stray beyond their strict competence. The presupposition internal to each mode is that it is absolute, that is, Experience itself. The practical man, the scientist, and the historian cannot help but attempt to reduce everything to their own favoured categories of explanation.

It is perhaps only in this sense that Oakeshott's frequent (and again quasi-Leibnizian) assertion that each mode is the whole of Experience viewed from an exclusive and limited standpoint is plausible (E 71, 101, 118, etc.). *Ex hypothesi* each mode must belong to Experience; but it surely cannot be said to 'view' Experience, since what it takes for Experience must, like any other object of modal thought, actually be its own creation. If the modes are opaque to each other, why should Experience be transparent to them (as they must be to it)? If a mode really were a perspective on Experience properly so called, it would destroy itself, for it would have adopted the viewpoint of philosophy. It would have become aware of its own relativity, and, at least by the postulates of *Experience and its Modes*, the bottom would drop out of its world.

Nevertheless, the modes need something to keep them true to their provisional character and (what is the same thing) to preserve them from irrelevance, that is, from trespassing on each other's territory. Irrelevance, for Oakeshott, is the cardinal sin. He often refers to it by the scholastics' name of *ignoratio elenchi*, understanding by that something like what Ryle means by a 'category-mistake'. Such an error would have been committed if, for example, a scientist claimed some special 'scientific' authority for his political convictions (J1 689f.; *cf* R 29n.); if one were to endorse or reject Darwin (say) purely on ethical grounds; or if (like Basil Fawlty) one were to 'punish' one's motor-car for breaking down by flogging it with a branch.

But how exactly can the modes be preserved from irrelevance

without surrendering all their authority, and hence their existence, to philosophy? Is it necessarily philosophy we should be looking to for a solution?

'The sign of all seriously undertaken thought,' says Oakeshott, is its 'freedom from extraneous purpose and irrelevant interest' (E 311n.). Surely this is intuitively obvious to any educated person. An historian needs no philosopher to tell him that there are some things he cannot say and still remain (while he says them) an historian proper. If he moralises about history he becomes a moralist - that is, he subordinates it to practical interests, no matter how admirable - while if he simply historicises morality he denatures it. And something similar is true of the scientist.

It seems possible, contrary to what Oakeshott says in *Experience and its Modes,* that modal thinking may after all be able to recognise its own proper limits from within. Following Oakeshott, I have so far spoken of the modes almost as though they were agents or individuals, but of course they are nothing of the sort. They are really languages, or rather what are nowadays called 'discourses', i.e. more or less self-sufficient meaning-systems within a broader meaning-system (Oakeshott uses the Victorian term 'universes of discourse' at R 150, 161, 164, 198). They 'become aware' of their limitations not on the authoritative say-so of philosophy, but because the individuals who 'speak' them are usually familiar with more than one. They are not fully opaque to each other, simply because they meet in individuals who 'come and go ... between a variety of universes of discourse' (H 23). Even if, as Oakeshott adds, their comings and goings are 'somewhat inconsequential', those individuals will retain some stable identity throughout.

An individual is more than the mere conduit for a bundle of insulated modal cables; for, qua individual, he is himself a 'world'. He need not, indeed cannot, confer upon the modes the unity he perceives in himself. All he needs is to perceive enough diversity among them to give him grounds for scepticism concerning the absolute claims of each; and it is precisely this scepticism which protects each from incursion by the others.

Seen in this light, Experience (in its monolithic, Absolute sense) becomes superfluous, even effectively 'transcendent'. It is at best something whose existence is optionally to be deduced or extrapolated from the empirical, self-subsistent fact of modal relativity. Oakeshott refers to Experience as the 'logical ground' of the modes (E 82), but does not remark that it could safely remain that alone. For what concerns us, if we are not philosophers, is not their relativity in comparison with 'truth' or 'reality', but simply their relativity in respect of each other (*cf.* R 206).

'Perhaps the only satisfactory view,' Oakeshott wrote, 'would be one which grasped, even more thoroughly than Hegel's, the fact that what we have, and all we have, is a world of "meanings", and constructed its philosophy without recourse to extraneous conceptions' (E 61). Might not 'philosophy' and everything connected with it in *Experience and its Modes* be precisely 'extraneous conceptions' of this kind? Oakeshott's later work certainly suggests the possibility. For there all quasi-transcendent absolutes either drop out of sight, or are reabsorbed into ordinary unphilosophical experience, and we are left with just such a self-subsistent 'world of "meanings"'. In 1967 Oakeshott writes as follows of Dilthey's *geistige Welt* (mental world), the 'civilised inheritance' (of beliefs, images, practices, 'facts' etc.) into which it is the object of education to initiate us:

> This is the only world known to human beings. The starry heavens above us and the moral law within are alike human achievements. And it is a world, not because it has itself any meaning (it has none), but because it is a whole of interlocking meanings which establish and interpret one another. (V 45)

Is the *geistige Welt* then not a new, present Whole, an all-inclusive Practice, perhaps, of which the specialist modes are offshoots? And secondly, if the 'starry heavens' and the 'moral law' (representing the 'natural' and 'human' worlds respectively - Oakeshott is alluding to a famous passage of Kant's) are both 'human achievements' and thus belong to the same *geistige Welt*, what need is there for Dilthey's distinction between the 'natural' and the 'human' (see Chapter 2 above)? Is 'nature' after all merely a human construct, and its independence - a supposition essential to its fruitful investigation - consequently an illusion? If the *geistige Welt* is really a unity, why does it require two distinct kinds of study?

I shall attempt to answer the first of these questions in due course. I raise the others merely that they shall not go unnoticed, for they must be excluded from present consideration on grounds not only of space, but also of their extreme difficulty.

4. Practice, Reason and Tradition

Oakeshott uses the word 'practice' in two senses. In *Experience and its Modes*, Practice is only one mode among others; in Oakeshott's later work, on the other hand, and most clearly in *On Human Conduct*, experience loses its logical unity and is replaced by a looser intercourse (or 'conversation') between various 'practices'. These 'practices' - some of which are far from 'practical', either in Oakeshott's original or in the everyday sense - are in fact the modes, split into sub-modes and given a new name.

Practice as a mode

Practical experience, or Practice, is the world (or Experience) seen, in Oakeshott's quasi-Spinozan phrase, *sub specie voluntatis*, i.e. under the aspect of will, volition and desire (E 258, 262, 308, 317). It is, quite simply, the world that we live in most of the time; not the *geistige Welt* in its entirety, but merely one of its contributory modes (or moods). Practice is peopled exclusively by individuals, that is, by selves and things: by discrete subjects pursuing (or avoiding), in fact or imagination, similarly discrete objects. Practice, like History, deals in designated particulars (E 147, 268), and thus differs from Science, which deals in generalizations (E 206); but it also differs from both Science and History in being actuated, not by disinterestedness (R 155-6, 159), but by its opposite, will.

Practice, however, is not predicated solely on egoism. Although 'in practical activity each self seeks its own pleasure' (R 215), 'pleasure' includes 'approval' and moral concerns generally. The world *sub specie voluntatis* comprehends the world *sub specie moris*, i.e. in its moral aspect (R 209). Not only individuality, but also morals, religion, politics and law (which constrain and condition it at every turn) belong to it. Nothing in Practice is indifferent or, in the scientific or historical senses, 'value-free'. Practice is governed not only by selfish, but also by unselfish, desire and aversion (*cf.* also H 124).

Desire, then, is simply my consciousness of the world's imperfection; and Practice, accordingly, is the class of actions, motives and conceptions bent on converting an existing to a preferred state of affairs (E 256f.). It should be added, with a side-glance at Hobbes on Felicity (R 184, R 253/A 81), that this conversion can never be final, because every satisfaction begets a further desire: 'permanent dissatisfaction (no matter how satisfied we may be with ourselves and our achievements) is inherent in practical experience' (E 304). (As we shall see, a major function of government in Oakeshott's view, as in Hobbes's, is to adjudicate or resolve the conflicts between citizens generated by this universal dissatisfaction.)

It is obvious from this account that Practice cannot be all-inclusive, and therefore cannot be the ground, origin, explanation or universal solvent of other modes. It may have social and biological priority (since we could not survive without it), but not logical priority. For that reason, it cannot be identical with Experience either, nor with whatever, in the later Oakeshott, supersedes it.

But (it will be said) does not the impulse, manifested in Science and History, to escape from the value-saturated world of Practice, itself constitute a desire, and are those 'theoretical' modes not therefore part of Practice after all? Are they not 'disinterested' in just the same way as disinterested moral behaviour, which does belong to Practice?

The answer (which Oakeshott himself does not provide) seems to be no. To be sure, the later Oakeshott is inclined to attribute a kind of non-practical 'value' to contemplative or quasi-contemplative activities such as art, history and science. And in order to do so, he is forced to narrow his conception of Practice, so that the more disinterested or more 'spiritual' aspects of morality are also excluded from it (see Chapter 7 below). But as far as *Experience and its Modes* is concerned, we may suppose his position to be roughly this: when, as an historian or a 'pure' scientist, I suspend my practical will, I suspend it absolutely, and enter a world - 'the past' or 'Nature' - which, being unalterable, is constitutionally impervious to will. On the other hand, when I behave in a disinterested or unselfish manner, I suspend my will only in respect of my own projects, and re-engage it in respect of others'. Here, as in love (*cf.* E 271-3), the will is not extinguished, but merely redirected.

One final point about Practice: the 'individuality' intrinsic to it is not the historic moral idiom or style which, as Burckhardt alleged, emerged definitively at the Renaissance, and which Oakeshott celebrates in his later writings. The 'self' or 'individual' of Practice is as old as Practice itself, which is the most primitive of the modes (R 197). We are plainly meant to understand by it any embodied will, any locus of desire, whatever. In this sense the 'anti-individual' or *esclave volontaire* (M 159f.; C 278, 303) is as much a 'self' or 'individual' as Montaigne or Goethe.

Separate practices and the forms of knowledge

So much for Practice and 'practical experience' proper. But when Oakeshott speaks of 'practical knowledge' (R 7f.) he is referring to something which belongs to any 'practice' (or 'activity', as Oakeshott usually calls it in *Rationalism in Politics*). 'Practical knowledge' may be found in any mode: the scientist, the historian and the artist all have their own versions of it.

Practical knowledge, to use Ryle's distinction, is 'knowing how' rather than 'knowing that' (*cf.* V 53f.). That is, it is a skill, and skills generally relate to means (of doing a thing). But Oakeshott's conception is less means-centred than Ryle's is usually thought to be. It extends also to a knowledge of ends, for example in the case of moral conduct. At one level, as we shall see later, morality for Oakeshott is simply a set of constraints; thus moral behaviour will merely be behaviour which observes those constraints. But at another, moral behaviour is an activity, a competence, even a form of self-expression. 'Knowing how to behave' is indeed a skill, but it also involves a serious conception, whether or not explicit or reflective, both of the end to which one's performance is directed and of oneself as part of that end (and also as an end generally). In this respect we might say that a 'knowing how' may sometimes incorporate a 'knowing that', though in the present instance the 'knowing that', being the whole motive force behind behaviour, far transcends mere inert information, and approximates rather to belief or conviction. (Cardinal Newman's distinction, roughly speaking, between 'notional' and 'real' assent.)

Generally speaking, what one 'knows how' to do is to engage in, find one's way about in, a given mode or activity: moral behaviour, religion, science, history, philosophy, cookery or motor mechanics as may be, and whether the said activity is a means or an end (though Oakeshott often treats even such apparently instrumental pursuits as cookery and motor mechanics as virtual art-forms, and thus as ends in themselves). Usually, of course, one cannot know how to do a thing without also knowing that such-and-such relevant to it is the case; but the 'knowing that' - which Oakeshott calls 'technical knowledge' - cannot by itself generate the ability to apply it. Technical knowledge is real enough but incomplete; it requires practical knowledge to make it effective. (The distinction is not unlike Carlyle's between the Mechanical and the Dynamic.) Technical knowledge can be formulated in rules, precepts, information, etc., and thus put into and got out of books. Practical knowledge, on the other hand, cannot. It belongs to what Polanyi has called 'the tacit component' of activity (a phrase echoed by Oakeshott at V 53). There is, however, nothing 'esoteric' about practical knowledge (R 8). It is acquired simply through experience, and in particular by apprenticeship, that is, 'by continuous contact with one who is perpetually practising it' (R 11).

No doubt when acquiring a simple knack (balancing on a bicycle, say) one learns purely from one's own experience. But a 'practice' is collective, and the experience embodied in it never merely one's own. To be sure, a practice, and practical knowledge, are learnt, and transmitted, by individuals (and indeed, in his later phase, Oakeshott seems somewhat inclined to regard the individual as the sole factor in the process; see C 86-7). But though those things exist nowhere but in individuals, as far as each individual is concerned a practice, like a language - which, as Wittgenstein argued, can never be 'private' - is a supra-individual thing. (If it were not, he could hardly be said to 'participate' in it.)

Tradition

Several things follow. First, a practice is traditional in a quite literal sense, in that the 'practical knowledge' involved is continuously handed on from the skilled to the unskilled: 'it would not be misleading,' Oakeshott says, 'to speak of it as traditional knowledge' (R 8). Secondly, a practice - which is to say a tradition - is never 'fixed and finished' (R 21, 31, 64, 102, 106, 126, 307; *cf.* C 64, 177). Though not in any foreseeable manner, it is always evolving. And this is because, thirdly, the individual is never a mere passive receptacle of tradition (as he might be of merely technical knowledge). He is not mechanically 'determined' by it, for it is transformed and extended by his own personal contribution. Indeed, without tradition, the individual would have (as with a language) no terms in which to express himself.

A tradition, then, is not so much (as the radical or 'progressive' would have it) a constraint on individuality, as its precondition. To empty the mind of its environmental filling - that is, of its practical knowledge, or what Burke defiantly called its 'prejudice' - in pursuit of an allegedly enhanced 'rationality' is in fact to empty it of everything important that makes it a mind. Nothing is left, one might suppose, but abstract intelligence ('brains'). Oakeshott, however, goes even further, implying that 'pure intelligence' actually signifies nothing at all (R 90). For it is central to Oakeshott's Idealist outlook that mind can never be independent of its objects, nor they of it. A mind is what it contains, and has no prior existence. To speak figuratively of objects, and the various modal worlds they inhabit, as being creatures of mind is misleading if it implies some kind of genuinely transitive relationship, for they and mind are in fact the same. (And of course they are no less 'real' for being mental constructs, since there is nothing outside mind by which to adjudge them 'unreal'.)

Rationalism and the sovereignty of technique

What Oakeshott calls Rationalism is the opposite of all this. The opening pages of the essay 'Rationalism in Politics' (1947) consist of an extended, brilliant and instantly recognisable 'Theophrastian character' of the Rationalist. I shall quote here about a sixth of it, not only for the substance, but also to give some idea of Oakeshott's writing at its graphic, eloquent best:

> There are some minds which give us the impression that they have passed through an elaborate education which was designed to initiate them into the traditions and achievements of their civilization; the immediate impression we have of them is an impression of cultivation, of the enjoyment of an inheritance. But this is not so with the mind of the Rationalist, which impresses us as, at best, a finely-tempered, neutral instrument, as a well-trained rather than an educated mind. Intellectually, his ambition is not so much to share the experience of the race as to be demonstrably a self-made man. And this gives to his intellectual and practical activities an almost preternatural deliberateness and self-consciousness, depriving them of any element of passivity, removing from them all sense of rhythm and continuity and dissolving them into a succession of climacterics, each to be surmounted by a *tour de raison*. His mind has no atmosphere, no changes of season and temperature; his intellectual processes, so far as possible, are insulated from all external influence and go on in the void. And having cut himself off from the traditional knowledge of his society, and denied the value of any education more extensive than a training in a technique, he is apt to attribute to mankind a necessary inexperience in all the critical moments of life, and if he were more self-critical he might begin to wonder how the race had ever succeeded in surviving. With an almost poetic fancy, he strives to live each day as if it were his first, and he believes that to form a habit is to fail. And if

we glance below the surface we may, perhaps, see in the temperament, if not in the character, of the Rationalist, a deep distrust of time, an impatient hunger for eternity and an irritable nervousness in the face of everything topical and transitory. (R 2-3)

The last two sentences are strongly suggestive of the poet Shelley, and perhaps lend colour to Oakeshott's allegation that 'the odd generation of rationalism in politics is by sovereign power out of romanticism' (R 7; *cf.* R 195). But what emerges from Oakeshott's ensuing list of typical Rationalist projects - ranging from the Rights of Man to 'national self-determination', and from Wells's World State to the 1944 Education Act (R 6; he could now add every Education Act since) - is a picture less of Romantic than of Enlightenment man. Indeed, one of contemporary Rationalism's godfathers was Shelley's father-in-law, Godwin, from whom Oakeshott selects this perfect gem of Enlightenment naïvety:

There must in the nature of things be one best form of government which all intellects, sufficiently roused from the slumber of savage ignorance, must irresistibly be incited to approve. (*ibid.*)

Evidently Godwin had been unimpressed by Montesquieu.

Rationalist politics, says Oakeshott, are the politics of 'perfection' and 'uniformity': 'there is no place in [the Rationalist's] scheme for a "best in the circumstances", only a place for "the best"; because the function of reason is precisely to surmount circumstances.' And this is true, not just in politics, but in any sphere - morals and education, for example - in which Rationalism has made significant conquests (see, e.g., R 32-6; 'The Tower of Babel', R 59-79).

The Rationalist is suspicious of tradition or practical knowledge, since the only knowledge he recognises is the technical kind. It and 'brains' together, working extraneously upon whatever 'problems' present themselves, make up, for him, virtually the whole of mind and its activity. Anything else will be either obstinately 'irrational', a shameful witness to the mind's imperfect autonomy, or the excuse for an occasional Orphic indulgence (see Oakeshott's quotations from Keynes on the supposed value of 'spontaneous outbursts', 'volcanic and even wicked impulses', etc., at R 94).

The instrumental mind

Oakeshott is hostile to the instrumental, problem-solving approach which has prevailed everywhere in the present century, from the architecture of the Bauhaus and le Corbusier (for whom a house was a *machine à habiter*), to the politics of 'social engineering'. The fallacy behind it is precisely that of supposing that mind is prior to and separable from its objects, and can be brought independently to bear upon them and to re-arrange them according to some 'rational', premeditated scheme. For the fact is that even when the mind supposes itself to be operating in this neutral, impartial fashion, it is not actually doing so. Either it is selectively reducing experience to some single favoured category - as when an architect ignores aesthetic in favour of ergonomic considerations, or reduces the first to the second - or it unwittingly admits into its deliberations precisely those intangible, but none the less concrete, considerabilities it originally purported, in the interests of 'rationality', to exclude.

Oakeshott gives a famous and amusing illustration of the latter phenomenon in the essay 'Rational Conduct'. The under-trousers for lady bicyclists to which Mrs Bloomer gave her name were a product of the Victorian fad for so-called 'rational dress', and advertised as such. According to Oakeshott, whoever actually designed them supposed themselves to be motivated purely by 'rational' - i.e. by anatomical and mechanical - considerations, and in particular to be making no 'irrelevant' concessions to fashion or appearance. Why, then, he asks, did they pause at bloomers and not go on to shorts, which (from the point of view purely of propelling a bicycle) are even more 'rational'? The answer is that, in spite of their 'unprejudiced' approach, the designers were still influenced by circumstantial, and hence 'irrational', considerations such as decency (i.e. behaviour appropriate for a lady in 1880), and built these into their design (R 81-3, 95-6).

The consequence was a garment more genuinely rational, because relevant to a wider, if unacknowledged, spectrum of considerabilities, than the one they actually thought they were designing. 'Human conduct,' Oakeshott concludes, 'may be said to be "rational" when it exhibits the sort of "intelligence" appropriate to the activity concerned.' (R 110). Rationality, in short, is simply another name for relevance; and from this follows the Aristotelian point (which the Rationalist, in his desiccated way, characteristically denies) that there is nothing intrinsically irrational about emotion (*cf.* C 40), so long as it is appropriate to its object. (Its appropriateness, of course, is not to be judged by any external criteria, but simply according to those locally available in the existing tradition of moral activity.)

The fantasy of abstract Reason

It is worth asking whence exactly the Rationalist can have got his dream of a wholly perspectiveless, universally applicable, Reason (which, we should note in passing, is not wholly unlike that attributed to the philosopher in *Experience and its Modes*; see, e.g., E 2). Its most obvious long-term source is Plato, for whom geometry was the paradigm of rationality. (Pascal, incidentally, criticised the *esprit de géométrie*, the geometrical outlook, as being inappropriate to the 'human' world, which is accessible only to the *esprit de finesse* - i.e. to taste, judgment, and experience.) According to Oakeshott, however, the fathers of modern Rationalism were Bacon and Descartes, in their search for an infallible method or technique of scientific discovery (R 13-20).

Neither, however, was directly responsible for the spread of Rationalism into other spheres, or for the belief (which Hayek has dubbed 'scientism') that science and scientific method alone were the key to all explanation. Those were the work of lesser men who, ignoring the scepticism which led Descartes eventually to abandon his project, took from him merely the project itself, converting it into the type of all intellectual and practical endeavour.

Rationalism, however, is not merely a set of beliefs about science. It exists whenever a set of reflective, self-conscious conclusions derived from any practice - which will include its 'technical' component - is promiscuously applied to any other. Of course, Oakeshott is opposed neither to technical knowledge nor to reflective thought *per se* (though practice, for him as for Ryle, always precedes reflection: see, e.g., R 118f., where he gives a further twist to Ryle's 'step-child' metaphor for the relations between the two; also H 120). But he does regard those things as much more prone than practical knowledge to detach themselves from their objects and to stray into *ignoratio elenchi*. The reflection appropriate (because native) to a given practice is tempted by its local successes to aspire to universal validity. The result is not only the invasion of politics, morals, history, etc. by 'science', but of science and history by religion, politics, or morals, in short, by Practice.

Two familiar examples might be the oft-heard calls for 'responsible' or 'committed' science, and so-called 'Whig history', *viz.* the interpretation of past events in the light of subsequent, and especially of present-day, political enthusiasms. In certain instances, such as the forcible imposition on Soviet agriculture of Lysenko's theories, or Hitler's promotion of 'Aryan mathematics' and the like, one can even perceive a double displacement, first from pseudo-science into politics, and then back again into real science. All such invasions are Rationalist in the extended sense. They not only generate intellectual confusion (since they spring from it), but may also succeed - and to succeed permanently they will usually need political backing - in completely destroying the activities they have colonised.

Ideology and its uses

What happens in every case is that an 'ideology' is extracted from the practice in which it is (or might have been) appropriate and applied, either to another, or across the whole field of practices. Why do ideologies arise at all, why does anyone want to believe in them, and how do they survive in the face of their own manifest incompetence?

A preliminary reply to the first question might be that purely at the local level ideologies answer to a genuine need for some readily-available technical knowledge. Furthermore, it is normal for human beings to reflect on what they are doing. When, as in science, their reflections issue in a set of provisional conclusions, to be fed back into (scientific) practice and corrected in the light of it, the resulting hypothesis is (or may be) valuable. But since, in science, the formulation of hypotheses is actually part of the practice, it may be doubted whether we have here a true example of ideology at all.

Nevertheless, Oakeshott more than once toys with the notion that scientific hypotheses offer an analogy with political ideologies of a corrigible, non-prescriptive kind, *viz.* those (such as British 'democracy') explicitly acknowledged to be 'abridgements' of an existing political tradition (R 119-21, 132; *cf.* R 25, 92, 101, etc.). He does the same in respect of the moral life. A society dominated by a 'moral ideology' (i.e. by 'the self-conscious pursuit of moral ideals') will be excessively subject to the dissatisfactions already inherent in Practice. It will suffer, as Oakeshott believes our own does, from 'an unhappy form of morality', a constant disruption of its unreflective, day-to-day moral certainties. There is an echo here of Hegel's 'Unhappy Consciousness' - roughly speaking, the condition of a pious but (in its very earnestness) sceptical soul unwilling to trust in the morally given or customary - and more than an echo of his distinction between *Sittlichkeit* (customary morality) and *Moralität* (precisely Oakeshott's 'moral ideology').

A 'mixed form of the moral life' (R 70), however, in which ideals, rather than mechanically dictating conduct, interact with and thus become part of it, is a lot more like the hypothetical-corrective model. It is also a lot more like what we normally understand by morality than is a wholly unreflective and almost equally mechanical following of custom. For us, surely, the latter hardly qualifies as morality at all.

Oakeshott, it seems, might agree. For although, given a choice of extremes, he clearly favours a morality of custom over a morality of abstract ideals, he nevertheless finds it liable to suffer from a 'want of moral sensibility' and a 'hollowness of moral character' (R 65). And one might remark also a shift in Oakeshott's sympathies away from a medieval 'morality of communal ties', which is a morality of custom, towards a post-Renaissance (and also, he thinks, Hobbesian) 'morality of individuality', to which the notion of intelligent decision is central (R 249-50/A 76-7; M 152-8; C 236f.). For clearly decision presupposes, if not the 'preternatural deliberateness' of the Rationalist, reflection at least of some kind.

Certainty and power

Our second question, as to why anyone should want to believe in an ideology, rather than merely use it for whatever provisional truth it may contain, may be answered, if not simply, at least in a word: certainty. No doubt many would refer the rise of ideology to the decline of religion, and to the consequent religion-shaped vacuum in experience which ideology then rushes in to fill. But such an explanation amounts to little more than a redescription (for perhaps, at least in some of its phases, religion is an ideology too). Others, such as Freud, or particularly Reich and Fromm, might invoke an 'unconscious' need for father-figures, a persistent infantilism, or a 'fear of freedom'. But such would-be 'deep' explanations themselves smack of ideology, and as such are wholly foreign to Oakeshott's historical, anti-naturalist manner of thinking (see his scepticism in respect of 'human nature', R 174; *cf.* also R 185, C 41, 93-5, V 64).

Oakeshott himself offers no explanation, though his comment about the Rationalist's need to be 'demonstrably a self-made man' offers a hint. The Rationalist could, if he wished, enjoy the provisional but immediate certainty of traditional knowledge. But he wants a superior kind of certainty, which shall at once affirm his 'freedom' by setting him above the common ruck of the thoughtless, and, in uniting him with some unconditional, transcendent or 'natural' order, shall both invest him with its authority and confer on him permanent existential security. Such a certainty must, like that which Descartes (and in another way Kierkegaard) sought, be wholly subjective: it must owe, or rather appear to owe, no debt to anything outside itself (a thing which must be impossible, if ideologies ultimately derive from practices). On the other hand, its subjectivity is in some strange way the guarantee of its objective validity.

If the foregoing analysis is plausible, it suggests two further things. First, it suggests why, among his various projects, the Rationalist almost invariably has a political programme on offer. What gives him the will, the right, and (as he sees it) the duty, to govern or to influence government is his privileged access to a wholly untainted, extra-political source of authority. And he has earned his right, he supposes, by his own 'free', or unaided, intellectual efforts (a claim which invariably rouses Oakeshott to irony: R 1, 35, 87). But it is just this assumption of privilege which signals the death of genuine politics, that is, of the politics of adjustment and negotiation. And in it, of course, we can perceive the germ of totalitarianism.

Secondly, it suggests that the Rationalist is obscurely related to his contemporary and antitype, the post-Renaissance 'individual'. Both aspire to 'freedom of thought'. Both perceive their surrounding traditions as inert. The Rationalist's answer is simply to reject tradition altogether in favour of some superior, absolute wisdom. But the 'individual' knows that, relative though tradition is, there is nothing outside it, and that innovation springs from nowhere else. His answer, therefore, is to revitalize tradition by exploring what Oakeshott (in speaking of political action) calls its 'intimations' (R 49, 58, 124, 132f.; C 237).

Of course, Rationalism too is a product of tradition, and, in a sense (since it has a history), is itself a tradition. But it is the product of a tradition (usually a scientific tradition) irrelevant to the activities it offers to supervise; and, when applied to them, Rationalism is a tradition without intimations, a changeless dream incapable of modification (as, e.g., a genuinely scientific tradition is not, since it is applied to, and perpetually modified by, its proper objects of investigation). Rationalism offers certainty, but a certainty which, being incorrigible by experience, is worthless. Nevertheless, its incorrigibility is Rationalism's chief attraction, and what commends it above all to the ignorant. The latter, lacking any practical knowledge of the activities they propose, or have been called on, to engage in, are driven to find a substitute in the shape of a Rationalist programme: what Oakeshott calls a 'crib'. In politics, Oakeshott observes, the greatest of all cribs is Marxism, 'composed for the instruction of a less politically educated class than any other which has ever come to have the illusion of exercising political power'. 'No other technique,' he continues, 'has so imposed itself upon the world as if it were concrete knowledge; none has created so vast an intellectual proletariat, with nothing but its technique to lose' (R 25-6).

Our third question, as to how ideologies survive, is now simply enough answered. They survive, not in spite of what Popper would call their unfalsifiability, but because of it. If they had the capacity to adapt themselves, they would cease to be ideologies and become again what they originally were, technical knowledge, evolving in parallel with practice because continuously subject to its criticism. But in severing themselves, first, from the practices which gave them birth, and, secondly, from the practices it has been decided they shall govern, they overleap practice altogether, and preserve themselves whole and entire until swept away by a general revulsion on the part of non-believers against their inevitable failures, and against the whole threadbare fabric of apologetics by which their failures have constantly to be explained away. In politics at any rate, it is precisely the remoteness of ideology from practice that can sustain it for so long: 'if you start being merely "intelligent" about a boiler or an electrical generator,' says Oakeshott, 'you are likely to be pulled up short by an explosion; but in politics all that happens is war and chaos, which you do not immediately connect with your actions'

(R 94; *cf.* R 28n.).

The politics of tradition

What view of politics specifically may be said so far to have emerged from Oakeshott's analysis of the matters dealt with in this chapter? It is clear, at any rate, that it cannot be Rationalist. For Rationalism presupposes that man's political, moral or social fulfilment must consist in the realization, within those spheres, of some extraneous, premeditated 'purpose'. Politics, for the Rationalist, is always implicitly activist and achievement-orientated, a matter of 'getting things done', and of using and extending to this end the power essential to government of any kind. Yet in Oakeshott's view politics is not a project to be executed, a problem to be solved, or a predicament to be transcended. It has no affinity with the scientific, military or commercial enterprises which have so often furnished the social engineer with his blueprints for a better world (R 121). Nor is it greatly amenable to supervision by ideologies of purely political origin, such as doctrines of Freedom, Equality, or abstract 'right'. For those are mere 'abridgements' of living political traditions, unnecessary (if natural) in the societies from which they arise, and generally useless or harmful when transplanted. (An example might be the imposition of Western 'democracy' on tribal Africa, where the supra-partisan consensus necessary for its proper working is lacking.)

Written constitutions and the like, Oakeshott thinks, are essentially ideologies of this kind, and he is accordingly sceptical as to their practical value. They are, at best, the equivalent of technical knowledge or of scientific hypothesis. (More than once he instances the Declaration of the Rights of Man and the American Declaration of Independence in this connection, though he later had second thoughts about their being Rationalist through and through: R 25-8, 120-2; *cf.* C 190, 244.) Indeed, and with the important exception of law, Oakeshott is generally sceptical about any visible institution (at least in its political applications) in which social man might seek to confirm his identity: the Church, for example, or the monarchy (consider his animadversions on what he clearly regards as the extravagantly 'ideological' Royalism and Anglicanism of the unnamed T.S. Eliot, R 183). For symbols, like ideals, can presumably always be resolved back into the tacit, concrete practices which they symbolise. These invariably have the structure of tradition. Traditions are the slowly-shifting foundation of social existence and, it seems, require no visible, or at least no directly political, means of support. Their maintenance, repair and development are spontaneous if unhampered by the 'planner'.

I have noted earlier that Oakeshott, though traditionalist, is not so in any nostalgic, reactionary, or restorationist sense. John Gray, indeed, has called him an 'uncompromising modernist', which echoes a phrase Oakeshott himself uses of Hegel (C 305n). The whole point about tradition is that it is dynamic and mobile. Oakeshott's view of it, accordingly, is essentially forward-looking. He shows as little interest in the origins of traditions as he does in the origins of the modes, saying only that 'activities emerge naively, like games that children invent for themselves' (R 137; and *cf.* R 237, on the spontaneous origins of 'Poetry'). It is sufficient merely that they exist and are familiar. From Oakeshott's standpoint the kind of conservative who wishes to recast the present in the image of a vanished past - a past, moreover, wrongly imagined to be static - would be scarcely less Rationalist than the radical and the progressive. Even of Hayek's neo-liberal *The Road to Serfdom* (1945), Oakeshott writes that 'a plan to resist all planning may be better than its opposite, but it belongs to the same style of politics' (R 21).

Oakeshott is a conservative, as he is a modernist, in the sense that change and the present are facts of life, and must first be accepted and understood as such before any further, more self-conscious change is possible: 'politics is not the science of setting up a permanently impregnable society, it is the art of knowing where to go next in the exploration of an already existing traditional kind of society' (R 58).

Oakeshott, by the way, says nothing of those ossified, and, until very recently, 'permanently impregnable' Rationalist polities of Eastern Europe. (Not surprisingly either, since, the USSR apart, they were only just being set up as he wrote.) Several of their features, however, are worth noting. First, though governed (or at least heavily buttressed) by a political ideology, they have allowed no 'politics' in Oakeshott's sense. Secondly, they have not been 'societies' at all, for under the rule of ideology society, its values and conventions - what some would call 'civil society', and others, culture - has been wholly banished from public life, and often extirpated altogether. Thirdly, where anything has survived (though it is hard for civil society to survive without political expression and support), political renewal can only come - is now coming - from these same 'relics of its own tradition of behaviour' (R 126). In this it is like moral renewal, which 'must make use of what is still unimpaired in the sufferer' (R 107). A civilised politics, in other words, depends on the political sphere's being made permeable to the cultural, whatever specific formal institutions that may be thought to entail (see Chapter 6 below).

Finally, it is obvious that an Oakeshottian conservative in a totalitarian state will find himself in an ambiguous position. For what is he to 'accept' or 'understand'? The existing power structure? Clearly he must do so in a superficial sense, for it is something which he cannot ignore and must confront. On the other hand, he must reject it in a deep sense, for it suppresses the civil order in which his intuitions of political rightness or justice are rooted. To that extent he will be, if only locally, a radical. But how will he stand in a free, genuinely representative polity like the post-war United Kingdom, which is still, even today, under the banner of official Conservatism, given over to various Rationalist projects, notwithstanding that those are consecrated to undoing the Rationalisms of a previous generation (*cf.* R 21-2, 36)? Oakeshott, I suppose, could only contend that reality must eventually triumph and that, until it does, the conservative who can command no hearing must simply hold his peace, or cultivate his garden.

But to return to the 'normal' case, that of 'an already existing traditional kind of society': it may be asked who exactly is to undertake or be entrusted with 'pursuing' its 'intimations'? As far as statesmanship goes, Oakeshott clearly prefers the traditional politician, born into a political family and thus equipped from the start with the appropriate 'feel' for politics, to the ambitious democratic *arriviste*, the academic Rationalist (Woodrow Wilson, say, or Harold Laski), or the radical demagogue (R 30; *cf.* R 24, 34-5). He does, however, concede that the 'new man' in politics, when faced with the collapse or unworkability of his schemes, will sometimes make a passable job of things by falling back upon his 'general experience of the world', that is, upon whatever practical knowledge he may have acquired in other activities such as business or Trade Union negotiation (though these, Oakeshott adds, are 'not always a good guide' and are 'often irrelevant': R 30, 94, 123).

From another angle, however, the 'pursuit of intimations' is something all of us, in our private and corporate activities, are engaged in. Here the task of government is emphatically not to decide where these activities should be going, but merely, in making, upholding, and amending the laws, to set and enforce the ground rules for their co-existence. Government is not only itself a practice, but also (ideally) the protector of all the diverse, self-chosen practices, and of the individuals who pursue them, which make up the life of a society (P 148, 150; R 184, 189, etc.). It follows that government cannot discharge this function if it presumes to participate or intervene directly in any activity, since (as a participant) its necessary impartiality, and hence its authority, will be impaired or even lost (R 193).

Oakeshott's politics amount to a kind of conservative liberalism or liberal conservatism. He has the conservative's respect for tradition, and the conservative's distrust of any individuality conceived, in the abstract liberal manner, as existing prior to the nexus of social activities, relations and traditions through which alone (on this view) individuality can emerge. On the other hand, he has the classical liberal's distrust of dirigiste or otherwise excessive government. Oakeshott's objections to socialism are easy enough to understand, resting on its officiousness, incompetence, and general indifference or hostility to freedom. (Freedom, for Oakeshott, is an historic achievement, not an abstract 'right'.) In this respect socialism is merely the epitome of Rationalism.

But Oakeshott's strictures might apply also to the strongly 'positive' government favoured by many traditional conservatives. This style of government involves what Lord Devlin called 'the enforcement of morals', the authoritative endorsement of some aspects of culture, and the suppression of others ('the persecution of the grosser forms of vice', in Fitzjames Stephen's phrase). Oakeshott appears to think that, so far from strengthening it, government actually compromises its authority whenever it seeks to embody any values beyond those unselfconsciously expressed or realized in the rule of law (see Chapter 6 below). He might be unsympathetic, therefore, to recent proposals in the United Kingdom for encouraging greater cultural homogeneity by (e.g.) favouring specifically Christian education in schools, or to the laws forbidding homosexual propaganda ('Clause 28'), even though these might be defended as attempts, albeit of a quasi-Rationalist kind, to counter certain manifest Rationalist abuses. Governing, he says, 'is a specific and limited activity', and 'not concerned with moral right and wrong'; 'its business is to keep its subjects at peace with one another in the activities in which they have chosen to seek their happiness.' A government 'which (in the old puritan phrase) "commands for truth" is incapable of doing so (because some of its subjects will believe its "truth" to be error)'; while 'one which is indifferent to "truth" and "error" alike, and merely pursues peace, presents no obstacle to the necessary loyalty' (R 189-90; *cf.* C 233, 284).

Earlier champions of this view of government, we may note, were Epicurus, Marsilius of Padua, and, up to a point, Hobbes. ('Up to a point', because for Hobbes a government might justly demand outward assent to any doctrine whatever, so long as its doing so conduced to peace.) Whatever its resemblance to liberalism, Oakeshott nevertheless regards this view of government as essentially conservative. He expounds it at greater length in *On Human*

Conduct, and accordingly I shall postpone further consideration of it, pausing here merely to observe that it is open to a number of *prima facie* objections. Not the least is that it may lead (in Oakeshott's own words) to a society 'so extravagantly diversified as to make an intelligently co-ordinated and civilized social life impossible' (D xix). In other words it has yet to be shown that a value-neutral government really is productive of peace. Does the subject look to government to protect his freedom of belief, or his beliefs themselves? If the latter, he will expect it to deliver them from the threat of competition (something he may accept in economic life, but which morals and religion perhaps cannot endure). Thus he may well be disappointed in what Oakeshott has to offer, and look elsewhere for alternatives. 'So natural to mankind,' as Mill said (without pondering the implications), 'is intolerance in whatever they really care about.'

5. The Modes (II): The Conversation Paradigm

I have more than once adverted to Oakeshott's move away from the Whole of *Experience and its Modes* towards a more pluralistic conception of the world as 'conversation'. Its first detailed exposition occurs in 'The Voice of Poetry in the Conversation of Mankind' (R 197f.), though the metaphor of politics as conversation goes back via 'Political Education' (R 125, 129) to 'The Political Economy of Freedom' (R 41; and see V 133, on 'The Universities', also from 1949).

Conversation in its literal sense is the opposite of argument or inquiry, which is the discursive idiom pre-eminently exemplified in science (R 197). And, though distinct from Practice (or as Oakeshott now calls it, 'practical activity'), which is governed by desire, argument has in common with it the principle, as Aristotle would say, of *proairesis* (purposive undertaking). Like Practice (or Rationalist government), argument is goal-orientated or, to use a later coinage of Oakeshott's, teleocratic (C 281, 322-3). As desire presses forward to satisfaction, so, through the dialectic of assertion and denial (R 304), does inquiry to 'truth', or at least to some kind of temporary conclusiveness. Like Practice, argument is a means to an end.

Conversation, by contrast, is an end in itself. It is endless also in being permanently inconclusive. It may be interrupted or adjourned, but it has no destination, being rather 'an unrehearsed intellectual adventure' (R 198). Since it has no substantive goal, but only the spontaneous enjoyment to be found in its exercise, any seriously eristic or competitive spirit is alien to it (there being nothing to compete for). Unlike Practice or inquiry, it prefers (in proverbial phrase) to 'travel' rather than to 'arrive' (see H 180; *cf.* C 324).

Conversation is of course hospitable to this or that propositional discourse or passage of argument, as it is hospitable to any contribution that does not presume to monopolize it; but in itself it possesses (like the *geistige Welt,* of which it is a microcosm) no ultimate propositional or referential significance. (Which is to say, not that it is 'meaningless' in the normal sense, but merely that its meaning, as with anything intrinsically valuable, is internal.) Conversation, in fact, is akin to play, as also to love and friendship, and to art; all these representing, in Oakeshott's view, either a partial or a total escape from the largely productivist or utilitarian ethos of Practice. (Oakeshott has spoken privately of his debt to Huizinga's *Homo Ludens* and to Valéry's Socratic dialogue 'Dance and the Soul'.)

Conversation is also Oakeshott's metaphor for the relation between all the 'diverse idioms of utterance which make up current human intercourse', the 'manifold' which together they compose (R 198). In other words, the real link between the modes is no longer a monolithic, substrate Experience perceptible only to the X-ray eye of the philosopher, but a dynamic, continuing discourse of discourses, or practice of practices, implied, echoed and openly acknowledged by many of them severally.

For example, conversation is not only the pattern of inter-modal relationship, but also (as just noted) a specific, literal activity that (as such) itself virtually constitutes a mode. It is the model, furthermore, of other activities such as education, academic life as a whole, and culture and civil society under a non-Rationalist government. Indeed, though Oakeshott does not say so, conversation could even be understood as the internal ethos of academic disciplines taken singly, including science and history, even though, structurally speaking, and seen from outside, those are argumentative in character. Finally, the parts of a work of art (the 'poetic images' of which it is composed) are also said to be 'conversationally' related, since 'they neither confirm nor refute one another' (R 246).

Oakeshott's new view, however, raises difficulties for his modal theory yet more radical than those remarked upon earlier. The modes, we are now told, 'enjoy an oblique relationship which neither requires nor forecasts their being assimilated to one another', and this relationship is one of 'acknowledgement and accommodation' (R 199, 304, 311). Some relationship there has to be, since a conversation presupposes some common basis, or matter, of communication. But Oakeshott nowhere precisely specifies it. What can it be?

Not unlike philosophy in *Experience and its Modes*, conversation imposes upon the participant 'voices' an awareness of their own relativity. Their exclusive claims to 'truth' are subordinated to 'keeping the conversation going', since if conceded they would destroy it (R 201; cf. C 202). But if the modes can communicate across their original boundaries, has not each forsaken its unique, untranslatable idiolect, and thus ceased to be a mode at all? And what then becomes of Oakeshott's vital conception of 'relevance', which depends on those boundaries' being preserved? Is not the central feature of a conversation the fact that in it nothing is irrelevant? And if so, does it make sense any longer to speak of relevance? Are we not landed simply in a promiscuous, supra-modal mish-mash out of which, because anything may be said, and because every voice has an automatic 'right' to be heard, little of any sense, coherence or value emerges?

I believe not, and that Oakeshott's conception can probably survive such objections. First, as already noted in Chapter 3 above, modes are channelled only through individuals, and most individuals, being conversant with more than one, are aware both of the modes' relativity and no less of the genuine claim of each to be taken seriously and protected against irrelevant incursions. If real-life individuals can live with this seeming paradox, so too can a philosophy that incorporates it.

Secondly, the modes do not actually have anything very substantial to 'say' to each other (if they had, they would compose a single mode). Once admitted to conversation, modal utterances are instantly qualified by their self-recognition as provisional, rather than as substantive or categorical, utterances. While not ceasing formally to affirm whatever modal 'facts' and presuppositions they contain, in conversation utterances also embody what T.S. Eliot (in speaking of 17th-century 'wit') called 'a recognition that other kinds of experience are possible'. The affirmation and recognition together make up, we may suppose, the 'determinate utterance' which each mode constitutes by its very existence (R 200). Some such interpretation, no doubt, can be put on Oakeshott's distinction between each voice's 'manner of speaking' - in respect of which each is 'wholly conversable' - and what is actually said (which may not be).

There is thus no reason, after all, why the conversation should degenerate into a welter of irrelevance. What each mode renounces on entering into conversation is not its integrity or identity, but merely its claim to exclusive validity (*cf.* H 11). And this concession is elicited, not by any rigorous wielding of the philosophic scalpel (as in *Experience and its Modes*), but simply by the existence of a 'meeting-place' (R 198) in which it becomes aware of others simultaneously both like and unlike itself.

I have called the Oakeshottian conversation a 'paradigm' not only because it is the pattern of modal interaction - the *geistige Welt,* in effect - but because it also, in microcosm, informs a number of local activities all connected, as it turns out, with the maintenance and transmission of the *geistige Welt*. Education, for example, is 'an initiation into the skill and partnership of this conversation in which we learn to recognize the voices [and] to distinguish the proper occasions of utterance' (R 199). In short, education is a matter of acquiring the practical knowledge appropriate to the 'conversation'. And this knowledge is not merely practical, but also specifically moral: a matter, essentially, of good manners, where modal assertiveness or dogmatism constitute the opposite (R 201).

Such knowledge, however, cannot be acquired in general or summary form. The *geistige Welt* is simply too heterogeneous - or as Oakeshott says, 'messy' (H 23n.) - to admit of any such reduction to principle. The 'judgment' or 'connoisseurship' involved in conversation can be learnt, in the first instance, only through mastering particular practices or disciplines (which possess the necessary homogeneity) in tandem with the informational or technical knowledge - the materials, one might say - appropriate to each (R 313, V

55f.).

Nevertheless, in the case of universities, each specialism offered for undergraduate study should be chosen for its intimations of a whole beyond itself (V 132). At all levels, ideally, a university conforms to the conversational model. Only so far as life is conversation can a university be said, or required, to reflect it. Oakeshott effectively counters the Philistine view that universities ought to reflect 'life' by implying either that they already do so (if we construe 'life' more broadly, to mean conversation), or else that a 'life' which does not reflect the university's naturally conversational ethos will be seriously impoverished.

A donnish, 'ivory tower' view, it will be said by those who have not considered its subtleties. But on any Oakeshottian reading, the current demand, first heard in the immediate post-war period (the date of Oakeshott's earliest educational essays), that universities should be made relevant to 'life' must rest on a gross misconception. What is meant is that they should be made relevant to Practice, that is, to current political, technological, and so-called 'social' enthusiasms (usually dignified as 'needs'), which are then wrongly identified with life as a whole. Barbarism supervenes, says Oakeshott, when any one voice dominates the conversation (R 201), and that is precisely what has happened in modern educational thought. Moreover, since the object of education (or at least of liberal education, which is here in question) is the study of things for their own sake, practical concerns are the one thing wholly extrinsic to it. In short, just as Rationalism is irrational, so nothing is less relevant (to education) than the Rationalist call for 'relevance'.

The conversational paradigm recurs in the moral life, 'practical' (for the most part) though that is. 'The merely desiring self,' says Oakeshott, 'can go no further than a disingenuous recognition of other selves; in the world *sub specie moris*, on the other hand, there is a genuine and unqualified recognition of other selves.' And 'selves in moral activity are equal members of a community of selves.' 'Moral skill,' he goes on, 'is knowing how to behave in relation to selves ingenuously recognized as such (R 210).' I shall have more to say about this, but for the moment it is sufficient to observe that moral behaviour, if we substitute 'modes', 'voices' or 'practices' for selves, is virtually identical (except perhaps in point of its greater homogeneity) to the mutual accommodation which characterises conversation. And above all, the accommodation of selves to one another, or rather the provision of conditions under which it becomes possible, is, as in Hobbes, the true object of politics as Oakeshott conceives of them. Hence politics also is concerned with conversation.

The ruler's concern, Oakeshott says, 'is with the "manners" of *convives*, and his office is to keep the conversation going, not to determine what is said' (C 202-3). Politics therefore turns out to be moral after all, though not in the simple Rationalist sense of dragooning citizens into the collective realization of somebody's moral 'goals'. The object - which is not a 'project', since the political engagement is as endless as the conversation with which it is concerned - is 'to keep the conversation going in terms of a civility among persons who have a propensity not always to be conversable' (Oakeshott's reading of Bodin, C 253). The only morality with which politics should be concerned, therefore, is that of civility, one of the central themes of *On Human Conduct*.

6. Agency, Association, and the State

In *On Human Conduct* Oakeshott no longer occupies himself with the modes specifically. The world now consists of various events or identified 'goings-on' which human beings are concerned to 'theorize' (C 1). (In these revised terms, a mode might be thought to comprise our dealings with this or that class or sub-class of 'goings-on' as defined by the specific quality and direction of our attention.) Theorization (i.e. reflection) is an endless pursuit, whose primary levels or 'platforms of understanding' are in no way invalidated or undermined by their successors (C 6, 26). We can either occupy a given platform, or move beyond it to the next. In so doing, as in Hegel, we become aware of its conditionality. But theorization, being endless, involves no progressive exhange of 'illusion' for 'truth', and never reaches any bedrock of absolute, unconditional understanding. 'Reductionism' is thus strictly impossible, because every reduction is susceptible of a further.

Oakeshott, in short, renews the attack on Rationalism from another angle. Like all of us in some degree, the genuine 'theorist' or philosopher is concerned to achieve a reflective understanding of things. Opposed to him stands the mere 'theoretician', 'intellectual', or *philosophe*. (The *philosophe* was the Rationalist's original title: see Oakeshott's 'The New Bentham', *Scrutiny*, I, 114f.)

Such a person is like the escaped cave-dweller in Plato's fable, which Oakeshott rewrites (Republic, VII; C 27-30). As in Plato, the representative of enlightenment returns to the Cave and offers his benighted fellows not merely superior, but absolute, knowledge, a 'complete substitute' for their 'conditional understanding'. Oakeshott, however, endorses the cave-dwellers' decision to send him packing. Had he, like the philosopher, told them merely that what they took for 'a horse' was really 'a modification of the attributes of

God' they might have been duly impressed, and gone their way. But when he tells them that his 'more profound understanding of the nature of horses' also makes him 'a more expert horseman, horse-chandler, or stable boy than they (in their ignorance) could ever hope to be', they understandably lose patience, particularly when they note that 'his new learning has lost him the ability to tell one end of a horse from the other'. (*Cf.* the opening of Dickens's *Hard Times,* in which the circus girl Sissy Jupe, who lives and works with horses, is put straight by the Rationalist MP Mr Gradgrind as to 'what a horse is'.)

Processes, procedures and performances

Of course the genuine 'theorist' might have, if not a profounder, at least a different understanding of a horse. The zoologist's horse is in its way no less 'real' than Dobbin, who knows me, whom I ride, and who comes to my call. Both are constructs, and both (up to a point) share the same features and obey the same 'laws'.

Above a certain level, however, they part company. *Equus caballus* is not an individual, but a species. It can (in theory) be ridden, but never by me. It has a name, but not one to which it will answer. It is not a horse, but a diagram of a horse. The distinction is clearer if we turn to human beings. From the scientific point of view human beings, like horses, stones, and waterfalls, are a collection of 'processes' (C 13). A process is a 'mechanical identity' (C 18, 92) abstracted from one or more 'goings-on'. Abstracted from the 'going-on' labelled 'human being', such an identity will be of interest to biology, medicine, and doubtless also chemistry and physics. But there is another category of identities, which Oakeshott calls 'procedures' (each being, in effect, the focus of a 'practice'), and it is these which human conduct or agency uniquely exemplifies.

A procedure is an exhibition of intelligence, and at every turn involves a decision (no matter how 'unintelligent' in the everyday sense) to do this rather than that (C 31). Conduct is intelligible only as procedure. It cannot be understood in terms of instinct, genetic inheritance, environmental pressures, infantile experience, etc., for all such explanations reduce it to a 'process' (C 20-25), and are thus merely *ignoratio elenchi* writ large.

These two 'orders' (C 12), processes and procedures, answer to the Kantian distinction between the realm of nature and the realm of freedom, i.e. between things impersonally 'caused' and things done for a reason (see C 235). They are, in effect, macro-modes, and, it seems, more radically immiscible than the modes themselves. (It does not appear, for example, that they can enter into any kind of 'conversation'.) If Oakeshott is right, therefore, enterprises which attempt to reduce procedures to processes, such as sociology and psychology (or more particularly their wayward offspring, Marxism and psychoanalysis), must simply be misconceived, not to say misbegotten. At least, they must be in so far as that actually is their object, and in so far as what they purport to explain as process is, in fact, conduct proper, rather than something either simpler, e.g. purely 'animal' perception and cognition, or more complex, e.g. the unintended social consequences of individuals' intentional actions (*sc.* conduct).

Of course, since Dilthey first made them, by no means all sociologists and psychologists have been unresponsive to criticisms in Oakeshott's vein. Oakeshott, however, says nothing concerning unintended consequences, which in fact form much of the specific subject-matter of the social sciences. It seems perhaps paradoxical or even monstrous that unco-ordinated intentional actions should exhibit in their aggregate outcomes an impersonal, law-like regularity akin to that which prevails in the physical universe. But it may be that there is no problem at all. For, if Oakeshott's treatment of economics in *Experience and its Modes* is any guide to his later thinking, there must be an unbridgeable categorical gulf between actions (procedures) and their unintended consequences (processes). Economics, he claims, is wholly scientific, and any attempt to resolve its generalities back into 'conduct' is simply an *ignoratio elenchi*. In his own words:

Economics is not an attempt to generalize human desires or human behaviour, but to generalize the phenomena of price. And the more completely it leaves behind the specifically human world, the more completely it discards the vocabulary which suggests this world, the more unambiguously will it establish its scientific character. (E 230)

What, then, is conduct, and what does understanding it entail? First, conduct is inseparable from reflection (C 31), of no matter how rudimentary a kind (I might, for example, do something simply because it is 'done', but that is still a reason for doing it). Conduct, however, is also distinct from reflection in that it invariably issues in a 'performance' (C 26, 33f., etc.), i.e. in something either done (an action) or said (a so-called speech act). Conduct, in short, is agency or utterance, the class of intelligent performances (and there are no others).

Being an utterance, a performance presupposes an audience or recipient. It belongs to a 'language', that is, to a practice (discourse, mode, activity), a given context of conventions and expectations. (It is not, however, specified by the practice to which it belongs, for then it would have been 'caused' rather than chosen.) And its performer's persona is dictated by his chosen practice (C 57): he may act, or speak (as he may also think), as father, colleague, citizen, chairman, friend, scientist, historian, philosopher or whatever.

Self-disclosure and self-enactment

All performances are 'self-disclosures'; some are also 'self-enactments' (C 41, 70f.). A self-disclosure is at once a response, either to others' utterance or to the mere existence of an audience, and an invitation to others to respond in kind (C 32, 38). In it, a self declares itself open (or still open) for business, announcing its pursuit of a desired object and asking for co-operation in securing it. The idea has a certain affinity with Collingwood's dialectic of question and answer (see his *Autobiography*), as it also has with Hegel's civil or 'bourgeois' society, the forum in which individuals reciprocally advertise and satisfy (or fail to satisfy) their wants (see *The Philosophy of Right*).

Self-disclosure is not in itself a 'moral' activity, though (as P.H. Wicksteed observed of economic activity) it is ineluctably subject to moral considerations. Performances of this kind are assessed by outcome, in terms of their justice or injustice, innocence or guilt. This is not, of course, a utilitarian question of their 'consequences'. The relevant question is only, 'Did they conform, or not, to the moral conditions prescribed?' (Or as Kant would have put it, were they *pflichtmässig*, outwardly conformable to the demands of duty, irrespective of the actual motive involved?) Self-enactments, on the other hand, are assessed according to whether the motives or sentiments concerned are honourable or shameful. What matters is not so much the bare action itself as the moral disposition or character it displays. Self-enactment is governed less by the compunction, 'What should I do?' (which may be purely prudential), than by the compunction in which it is finally subsumed, 'What sort of person do I want, or ought I, to be?'

As Oakeshott points out, for some thinkers, notably Aristotle and Kant (with suitable qualification, he could have added Nietzsche), only the last is truly a 'moral' consideration (C 71). As an anti-essentialist, however, he differs from Aristotle (as also from Marx) in denying that there is any 'ultimate or perfect man' or (as Marx would say) 'species-being' which it is our business, or destiny, to realize; the agent, he says, 'has a "history", but no "nature"' (C 41; *cf*. V 64, R 26n.).

Virtue and ethics

Self-disclosures are subject to considerations of acceptability, self-enactments to considerations of 'virtue'. There is in virtuous self-enactment something gratuitous or supererogatory, a kind of finesse, delicacy, or taste (something to which Oakeshott shows Hobbes, contrary to conventional opinion, to have been sensitive: see R 289/A 120f., and *cf*. C 77). This has led some in the past (myself included) to accuse Oakeshott of a kind of aestheticism, of a self-centred, narcissistic preoccupation with moral style at the expense of moral substance. (And it must be said that Oakeshott's 'virtue', centred on the individual as such, is a good deal more colourful and interesting than Kant's lofty conception of duty, which, binding as it does all rational beings indifferently, seems imaginatively meagre by comparison.)

I no longer think, however, that this accusation (a version of the 'Tory dandy' charge) can be sustained. Certainly for Oakeshott virtue has an 'aesthetic' dimension, which mitigates the frustrations attendant on practical activity, and even approximates it (virtue) to religion, which now seems (like Poetry) to have transcended Practice (C 73-4, 81f.). But Oakeshott goes to considerable lengths to distinguish virtue both from a person's 'own good opinion of himself' and from his self-approving 'conscience' (a thing acutely criticised, incidentally, by Hegel). Virtue delivers us not from the moral constraints to which self-disclosure is subject, but only from its prudential considerations; from the anxiety as to whether our projects will succeed, and from the disappointment consequent on their failure. And, if it cannot deliver us from our mortal condition, it can at least ensure that we accept it, and meet death gracefully. Virtue in the end is a self-imposed requirement on the agent's part 'of thinking about himself as he should while doing what he ought'. It is a matter not of self-conceit, but of self-respect and integrity, of the Platonic 'care of the soul'.

The account of morality given in *On Human Conduct* is dense, complex, painstaking and extremely subtle, so the reader in search of further enlightenment on this topic must henceforth be referred directly to Oakeshott himself. Nevertheless, one final feature of it may be remarked. For Oakeshott, moral rules are not positive injunctions to do or to forbear. They are neither retrospectively-applicable criteria of good behaviour, nor ideals to be translated into substantive action. Rather, like ideology, they are 'abridgements' of an already existing practice or tradition of behaviour (C 66; *cf.* R 25, 92, 101 etc.). What they do, Oakeshott says, is 'to concentrate into specific precepts considerations of adverbial desirability which lie dispersed in a moral language' (a fair specimen, incidentally, of the later Oakeshott's muscle-bound, Laocoönesque prose).

In other words, whatever authority moral rules possess is not final, for they are incompetent to prescribe to a particular agent what precisely he must do in a particular case, and in any event frequently conflict. Their authority derives, rather, from the authority of the complete moral practice or 'language' from which they have been abstracted. And that (presumably), despite its long-term mobility, and the fact that its deliverances are plural and far from unambiguous, is absolute, simply because it is not grounded, in turn, in anything else. Moral rules are really 'prevailing winds which agents should take account of in sailing their several courses' (C 70).

That, however, is not to say that morality is relative, only that its so-called rules or principles are. Nor does it mean that we can simply make up our values as we go along, or dignify our subjective preferences with the title of morality (perhaps appealing the while to some liberal absolute such as the individual's 'right to choose'). In short, there is nothing in Oakeshott much resembling either the fashionable 'situation ethics' of the 1960's or their Bloomsbury forebears.

In the end, and despite their anti-teleological and anti-essentialist thrust, Oakeshott's ethics are much like Aristotle's (and, many would say, Hume's). What should be done in a given case is a matter for *phronesis* or practical wisdom, the 'knowing how' of the morally literate agent immersed in practice. And precisely because morality is a practice, that is, a shared vernacular language, the acts and judgments of the *phronimos* (the man endowed with *phronesis*) possess an objective validity and intelligibility which redeems them equally from the capriciousness or self-reference of 'conscience', from the immoralism which affects to dispense with it (*cf*. H 135), and from the self-dramatizing subjectivity of the 'authenticity'-seeking existentialist. The real significance, perhaps, of Oakeshott's assimilating the higher reaches of morality to the aesthetic (see Chapter 7 below) is that they thereby attain to the genuinely 'objective' status which the 'aesthete', who reduces everything to private sensations or 'states of mind', would finally have to deny even to art.

Contingency as a principle of understanding

It will be as well here to glance at the question raised earlier, of how conduct is to be understood. As we know, conduct consists of 'performances', and every performance occurs within, and is meaningful only in relation to, a 'practice'. According to Oakeshott, a practice can be expressed in a 'theorem', a performance not (C 91). That is to say, although a practice can be analysed in terms of certain rules or principles, a specific performance within it cannot be deduced from them, nor (consequently) wholly explained in terms of them. Practices do not specify performances, any more than a language determines a particular utterance.

Once we have identified the practice to which it belongs, our understanding of a performance begins at the point of utterance, in its relationship to its prior circumambient conditions. This relationship is one of 'contingency' (C 101f.). By 'contingency' Oakeshott does not mean what J.B. Bury meant in his essay on 'Cleopatra's Nose', *viz.* arbitrariness or chance (E 133). (The allusion is to Pascal's uncharacteristically silly remark that if Cleopatra's nose had been shorter the whole course of history would have been different; silly, because why stop at that particular variable? So would it if she had never lived, or if omnibuses had been invented and Antony had been run over by one, etc., etc.: in short, the whole course of history would have been different if it had been different.) Oakeshott means by contingency something etymologically much more literal, *viz.* 'touch', 'fit', or 'contiguity' (C 104; H 94, 113-4). What this amounts to, at least in part - though as his own analysis shows, it is extremely hard to define precisely - is that every performance has to be seen in the context of its immediate circumstances, not, however, as strictly caused by them, but rather as provoked by them, as an intelligible human response to them. (And of course those circumstances, if themselves performances, will be similarly intelligible, and so on, in ever-widening circles.)

Contingency is an important concept in the later Oakeshott for two reasons. First, it is the fundamental relation between historical events (see next chapter) and thus the primary object of historical understanding, which is essentially narrative (C 107; H 94-5, 114; and *cf.* 'The Activity of Being an Historian', R 137f., where 'contingency' first makes its appearance). And secondly, it is the model of all rational, rather than Rationalist, political innovation (C 179-80; *cf.* R 172, J1 488). It may seem odd, but the most desirable actions appear to be those most easily intelligible to future historians, in other words those maximally continuous with their immediate antecedents. (Thus 'a war to defeat a recognizable mischief', for example, is clearly more 'intelligible' than a Rationalist 'war to end all wars': J1 352.) But this is no odder than the suggestion that life and the university share a common conversational structure. For utterances in conversation (as in argument) are also primarily related in terms of contingency.

Enterprise association

Conversation and argument are the implicit paradigms of the two ideal types of human association identified and expounded in the second part of *On Human Conduct*. These are 'civil' and 'enterprise' association respectively. I shall begin with enterprise association.

Self-disclosure is the basis of what Oakeshott calls 'transactional association' (and Hegel, 'civil society'), the reciprocal satisfaction of substantive wants (C 112, 175; H 121f.). Enterprise association is a version of transactional association, consisting of the joint satisfaction (or pursuit thereof) of perceived common wants (in this respect it is not unlike Tönnies' *Gesellschaft*). These satisfactions need not be material or economic - they might equally be moral, religious, political, or even athletic or recreational (a golf club) - but they are 'substantive'. (The epithet 'substantive' is nowhere defined, but seems less obscure than its regular Oakeshottian antithesis, the 'formal'. For example, Aristotle's *eudaimonia* or practical happiness, which results from virtue, is said to be 'formal' rather than 'substantive', despite the fact that its possessor obviously experiences a kind of 'satisfaction'. Perhaps Oakeshott means that, like 'pleasure' for Bishop Butler, it is too general to be a discrete object of desire. It is still not clear, however, why that makes it 'formal'. See C 118-9n., and *cf*. 53, 61.)

Enterprise association, then, is purposive association, and as such a means to an end. The following are its key features (C 114f.). First, it is voluntary, chosen by the associates individually (there being no genuine 'collective choice', for only individuals can choose). And since it is continuously sustained by choice, each associate retains a right of exit (unless, one supposes, he has voluntarily renounced it, say by a vow).

Secondly, enterprise association (like self-disclosure) is governed externally by moral rules and constraints. It observes them, but it is not constituted in terms of them, nor yet in terms of its own internal rules, which are purely instrumental to its purpose (that being the thing in terms of which it is constituted). Being instrumental, therefore, the rules of an enterprise association are readily modifiable by the associates whenever they are observed to be impeding its purpose, and can be changed without prejudice to the association's character.

Finally, an enterprise association will be 'managerial': the associates either decide collectively, or depute some of their number to decide, to do this rather than that in pursuit of the association's 'policy', and in response to the contingent circumstances, in the same way as an individual pursues his 'wished-for satisfactions'. Such continuous 'management' is necessary because, just as a rule cannot determine its local applications, so the policy of an enterprise association cannot itself determine how it is to be implemented in particular cases.

Civil association

Enterprise association, says Oakeshott, is 'the most familiar of all durable human relationships', and that is doubtless one reason why it has so often been taken as the model of, or for, political association generally (it is, of course, the principle behind political parties). But for Oakeshott the ideal political relationship, which is also peculiar to politics, is civil association. Being an historic achievement, however, it is feasible only in societies which have already in some measure learnt the appropriate political 'manners', *viz.* 'civility', and indeed is abstracted from their practice. Though not in itself pre-political, it could be regarded as giving voice, or scope, to an independent cultural value which politics exists to protect.

Civil association is association in terms not of wants or purposes, but (as in conversation) of generally-acknowledged rules. These rules, considered as a body, Oakeshott calls *lex*, meaning not this or that law, but 'the law' or law generally at any given time; the political order which sustains them, and which they reciprocally reflect, he calls *civitas* (roughly, 'the state', or rather a specifically 'civil' conception of it). The whole practice, of which *lex* forms the rules, is *respublica*. It may be observed that, just as science is an intrinsically hypothesis-making practice, so *respublica* is an intrinsically rule-making and rule-observing practice. Thus, though in general a wholly 'moral' phenomenon, it differs from morality proper, whose rules are secondary 'abridgements'.

Legal rules differ from moral rules, though the subject's obligation to observe them is (like any other) a moral one. In a moral community (that is, a collection of people who speak the same moral 'language') the rules - or rather, the implicit moral norms they purport to articulate - may of course change spontaneously or otherwise come to be modified; and they may equally be debated. But they are not formal rules, and therefore cannot be deliberately revised, repealed, or replaced (there is, for a start, no procedure for so doing). They rely for their force solely on the subject's approval, that is, on his fundamental conviction of their rightness (C 160-1). Once this lapses, they lose their force (as they are bound to do if subjected to continuous debate: 'ceaseless criticism never did anyone or anything any good', V 115).

A legal rule, however, does not depend on the subject's approval of its morally substantive content. What (under civil association) it depends on is his recognition of its formal authority, that is, that it has been properly made and proceeds from an authentic source (H 130f.). He recognises, in other words, that even though he may morally disapprove of it he is nevertheless obliged (and not merely compelled) to obey it. He is obliged to obey this law, not because it is in itself a good or a just law, but because it is part of *lex* as a whole, which he is obliged, and (in the normal case) regards himself as obliged, to obey.

The subject's inward assent, of course, cannot be enforced. His outward conformity, however, to *lex*'s prescriptions can; and it is doubtless on account of the inherently compulsory nature of *lex*, and the dangers involved in its being generally perceived in that character alone, that every effort is made to ensure that its prescriptions do, in fact, coincide with his moral sentiments. Nevertheless, the 'moral sensibility' involved in civil association is assumed to be 'educated', by which Oakeshott of course means not that it should reflect the prejudices of the so-called educated class, but that it should be capable of discriminating between those moral desirabilities which it is, and those which it is not, reasonable (or feasible) to require the law to impose (H 160). (It would, for example, be absurd, not to say impossible, for the law to require 'virtue' of its subjects.)

The members of a civil association, therefore, are capable not only of recognising that there is a boundary between 'public' and 'private', but also (and whether or not they themselves enjoy any legislative powers) of recognising where it should be drawn. To maintain the coincidence of law and sentiment is the role of politics and legislation, but of course (as with moral disputation) too much of either, like too little, will simply erode the credibility of the whole system and end by destroying it (R 190; C 138-9). The central principles of a society ruled by law are continuity and consensus (R 48-9, 128).

Oakeshott's exposition, in both *On Human Conduct* and 'The Rule of Law' in *On History*, is exceedingly compact. Nevertheless, as I understand it, it answers fairly accurately to the intuitions of the ordinary law-abiding citizen. There is no space to go into all Oakeshott's jurisprudential reasonings concerning legislation, adjudication, law-enforcement and administration, and their analogues (where appropriate) in enterprise association (Oakeshott, incidentally, wrote on jurisprudence as long ago as 1938, in the journal *Politica*). However, one or two are worth mention here.

Law and authority

First, what makes *lex* authoritative? It is not utility, because utility could never constitute a moral reason for obedience. If *lex* secures certain desired goods to us (life, liberty, etc.), it does so because we are already disposed unforcedly to obey it; in other words, that it endures is in virtue of our recognising its authority. (Here Oakeshott diverges from one of his masters, Hobbes, and approximates to Hume, for whom consent proceeds from perceived legitimacy, and not legitimacy from so-called consent, let alone 'contract'.)

Then again, *lex* as such does not derive its authority from anything transcendent: neither from 'will' nor from 'right' (of the sovereign, 'leader', subject, law officer, collectivity, majority etc.). Nor is it authoritative in virtue of any 'social purpose' or moral ideal it might serve; for (we might add) not only does that make it instrumental, but it would also (like the rules of an enterprise association) be constantly defeasible in the face of ad hoc 'policy' decisions.

This, indeed, is actually what happens when a *civitas* finds itself at war, or otherwise seriously threatened; for then it becomes a temporary enterprise association, whose 'goal' is survival (C 146-7). And even in normal times (though Oakeshott himself does not say so) the survival of *lex* may rest upon its readiness to yield, in emergencies (the sole occasion, in Hegel, for the constitutional monarch's executive intervention), to *raison d'état*. This tiny nucleus of enterprise association at the heart of civil association, however, must surely be counted as part of it (somewhat as the law-abiding individual retains the right of self-defence in emergencies).

It surely does not, as some of Oakeshott's critics (notably D.D. Raphael) have thought, invalidate the whole distinction. In any case, as Oakeshott stresses, these are ideal types of association, never, in real-life politics, appearing in wholly unmixed purity.

Finally, Oakeshott rejects the idea (unattributed, but actually Kelsen's) that the authority of law derives from some anterior 'basic norm', e.g. 'the constitution' (C 151). (In fact Kelsen's *Grundnorm*, or basic norm, is not a thing but a belief, to the effect that the constitution, the monarch, the people, or whatever it may be, is supreme.) For Oakeshott, it might be said, *respublica* is its own *Grundnorm*: like any practice, and the all-inclusive *geistige Welt*, it is self-sustaining, self-justifying, or (in Aristotelian phrase) 'self-sufficient' (see C 150-4). Such an account of authority is no more mysterious than Kelsen's, and in many ways less so. It is surely more plausible that cultural, moral and legal systems should severally compose 'a whole of interlocking meanings' (V 45, and see Chapter 3) and nevertheless collectively 'hang in the air', than that any item or part thereof, such as a 'constitution' (or a 'basic norm' pertaining thereto), should be left to do so by itself.

Civility and culture

Common subscription to *lex* is by definition the bond of civil association (C 149). And it is a moral bond, between citizens qua citizens (*cives*). But because it is 'formal' (i.e. a bond between persons in a particular public capacity) it is necessarily indifferent to their 'private' (or perhaps 'substantive') moral beliefs and behaviour. And here, of course, as in Mill, there is much room for equivocation as to what is, and is not, truly 'public'; be that as it may, Oakeshott describes the 'so-called moral neutrality of civil prescriptions' as a 'half-truth', because civil association is itself 'moral' (C 175).

Cives are not allies in a cause, partners in an enterprise, beneficiaries of some symbiotic arrangement, lovers, intimates or even friends. I am bound in 'civility' to those with whom I have nothing else in common, to those I have never met, even to those whom I happen personally to dislike, in just the same way as I am bound to obey particular laws of which I happen to disapprove. It might be thought that civility - which amounts really to a kind of minimal mutual respect - is a rather tepid, uninspiring basis for political society; it resembles, Oakeshott says, the dilute friendship or 'watery fidelity' thought by Aristotle to prevail between citizens (C 110, 147). It is certainly not the stuff of which 'mass movements' are made (and so much the better, Oakeshott would say).

Nevertheless, it is recognisably a real thing, which has motivated people to hazard their lives willingly in its defence. The enthusiasm on which it draws is not that of citizens for each other personally (for most are total strangers), but of all citizens for that common way of life of which *lex* is at once part, an expression, and the guarantee. A *civitas* need not be culturally homogeneous (though doubtless a degree of homogeneity will help): Oakeshott, as we have already seen, regards nationalism and the so-called 'nation' state, like 'race', as essentially a Rationalist fantasy (R 6), and he is equally unsparing with his scorn in *On Human Conduct* (C 188, 191, 279, 296n.). The only homogeneity which counts, and which is essentially 'cultural', consists in a common disposition to value *lex* above one's local cultural identity. It is presumably only when the latter acquires more importance in the subject's eyes than the law which (in fact) protects it and allows it to flourish, that cultural difference poses a threat to civil association (as it most notably does when religious).

What is really in question is not radical 'cultural diversity', but something which may equally be found under conditions of cultural homogeneity, *viz.* the detachment of the citizen's substantive moral approval not merely from this law or that (which is only to be expected), but from enough of the ensemble to call *lex* itself into question (see R 190). The *lex* which engages its subjects' loyalty is not any old *lex*, but one which on the whole generates laws agreeable to their moral intuitions and possesses sufficient flexibility to advance or retard itself accordingly. ('A state without the means of some change,' said Burke, 'is a state without the means of its own preservation.')

In other words, if *lex* is truly to exist - i.e. be acknowledged as such by its subjects - it must keep in step with them and (perhaps especially) not attempt, in the manner of modern liberal societies, to bully them into enlightenment. (A thing which is not as paradoxical as it sounds: for if the law declines, on 'liberal' grounds, any longer to protect the normal citizen against things offensive to his sense of decency or right, it oppresses him, at least in his own eyes, as surely as when it proscribes his own 'illiberal' sentiments, or countenances their unofficial proscription.) It seems, in the end, that *lex*'s necessary 'indifference' to its subjects' moral beliefs signifies only a reluctance to defy or to interfere with them. If so, Oakeshott's position turns out after all to be genuinely conservative. The difficult distinction between 'private' and 'public' morals, which Mill's apparently clear formulation of it in terms of 'self-regarding' and 'other-regarding' actions only served further to obscure, is ultimately decided not by governments or political thinkers but by subjects. If the latter expect morals to be enforced, then a government which disregards their wishes, or attempts to impose some other morality upon them (R 186-7), puts itself, and *respublica*, in jeopardy. On the other hand, it will also be an 'uncivil', and above all an unwise, society which calls for a degree, or kind, of conformity to which any sizeable minorities in its midst may be expected to take serious (and not merely selfish) exception. To make it impossible for citizens who would otherwise do so to identify themselves with *lex* is to free them, in their own eyes, from any obligation save that which they feel to their own 'community', and to store up obvious trouble for the future.

Policy and constitution

All these are matters, finally, for tact, negotiation, experience and trial-and-error, in short, for 'the pursuit of intimations'. Oakeshott, as one might expect, has little, and in some cases nothing, to say about them, being concerned with principles rather than prescriptions (see, however, R 135, 4). Indeed, he is notoriously reluctant throughout to advance any 'policy', since unlike the Rationalist he believes that none can be 'mistake-proof', in any practice whatever (R 136; C 180).

Nor does he tell us which precise constitutional arrangements are most suited to civil association. Civil association obviously entails authoritative but legally accountable 'rule', rather than dynamic 'leadership' or discretionary 'management'; but, having emerged historically from many different constitutional arrangements, it specifies none in particular. It presupposes some means of ascertaining subjects' wishes; it may even suggest that the most effective would be some form of parliament; but whether or not such a body ought to be 'democratic', and what its powers (if any) should be, are not questions which theory alone can decide. Civil association, like monarchy (which it does not, of course, entail), is 'above' day-to-day politics (C 164-5). For, as Mill observed in his essay on Coleridge, in every society held together by allegiance rather than by force, there must be 'something settled, something permanent, and not to be called in question; something which, by general agreement, has a right to be where it is, and to be secure against disturbance'.

The final part of *On Human Conduct*, 'The Character of a Modern European State', is a dazzling feat of historical compression illustrating the emergence of two alternative conceptions of the state, one corresponding to civil and the other to enterprise association. Criticism of its multitudinous historical detail is a matter for the professional; I shall confine myself to pointing out whatever has not so far been mentioned, or throws a new light on what has. This essay is by far the raciest and most immediately intelligible part of the book. It presupposes little or no acquaintance with the two previous sections, recapitulating as much of them as necessary; much of its substance, indeed, had already appeared as a self-subsistent article, 'The Masses in Representative Democracy'.

Societas and universitas

Classical, mediaeval and early modern theorists, Oakeshott says, found analogies of the state in two concepts from Roman private law, *societas* and *universitas* (C 199-205). *Societas* was the relationship between (e.g.) 'friends or neighbours, suitors to a court or speakers of a common language', even between human beings as such (as fellow-subjects of Natural Law); in other words, between people who, in virtue of the relationship to which they were parties, were morally obliged to treat each other in a certain way. Members of a *universitas*, or 'corporation aggregate' (i.e. a partnership in a common purpose), would have had the same moral obligation, but independently of their membership of the *universitas*. Within it (we might suppose) they were merely expected to behave in a certain way, observe certain rules, obey directives, etc., and if unprepared to do so they had either to leave or to be expelled. In other words, their relationship (at bottom) would be not moral but instrumental (and also voluntary). Examples of *universitates* are churches, guilds, boroughs, and (of course) universities.

Useful though it may be, the analogy with the state in each case is far from watertight. This is largely because the Latin terms denote associations which (at least notionally) begin in the 'private' sphere, whereas the state is by definition 'public' and above all compulsory. And secondly, there are a great many loose ends left in the implicit parallels with civil and enterprise association. I can do no more here than remark a couple; they do not invalidate Oakeshott's distinction (which is, after all, his own and not some medieval theorist's); and he himself has noted the first.

To begin with, civil association is compulsory, whereas friendship (which belongs to *societas*) is voluntary (though as Burke observed of marriage, the duties pertaining to it are not). Then again, though a university has a common purpose (disinterested inquiry), its conversational ethos is surely more that of *societas*. And finally, a church has a common purpose (worship, salvation, etc.), and is thus a *universitas*; but also, because in its members' eyes it is a moral purpose, they will unquestionably see themselves as a moral and not merely as an *ad hoc* association. Furthermore, its members do not belong purely in a certain capacity (e.g. as citizens); rather, it embraces their whole existence, so that each is engaged as a complete person. To use Tönnies' distinction again, a church is a *Gemeinschaft* (community).

Oakeshott seems inclined to discount this feature of at least some enterprise associations. One whose common purpose is moral will always regard itself, in the last resort, as entitled (like a threatened 'minority') to refuse its assent to *lex*. And others, whatever their original purpose, have a natural propensity rightly or wrongly to invest themselves with a moral character (e.g. trade unions with their 'solidarity'). It is perhaps because such associations may thereby come to regard themselves as 'above the law' that every effort has been made, historically, to bring them within it by giving them a 'legal personality', which at once gives them formal recognition and makes them answerable in law for their actions.

Oakeshott would obviously acknowledge the force of the latter consideration (answerability). But it seems unlikely that he could easily countenance the former (recognition), with its implicit admissions, first, that enterprise associations may either develop, or possess intrinsically, internal moral relations; secondly, that (especially when thus reinforced) they may constitute a serious challenge to law, civil association, or indeed to any government whatever (see, however, R 53-4, on 'syndicalism', i.e. trade unions); thirdly, that simply as a matter of *raison d'état* such powers may have to be appeased, in the hope that their conditional assent may eventually modulate into unconditional; and lastly, that appeasement, since it has often consisted (and certainly did in the case of mediaeval universitates) of the grant of various charters, monopolies, privileges, immunities, etc., may involve tolerating something ruled out by civil association, *viz.* inequality before the law.

It must be said that Oakeshott's treatment of the politics of power, prudence and calculation, even in 'The Political Economy of Freedom', is somewhat sparse. Indeed, it is a tribute to his humane, civilized outlook to say that in his writings the darker side of politics - violence, coercion, punishment, *Realpolitik*, 'the noble lie' and the rest - barely gets a look in, though one can hardly suppose him to be unaware of its importance.

The state as person

The *universitas*, Oakeshott says, was a *persona ficta*, a creation of authority, and subject to its inspection (though as his obvious sources Gierke and Maitland had originally pointed out, this was essentially a matter of imposing legal responsibility upon associations already understood by their members to be moral agents simply on account of their corporate identity, whether or not their professed purpose was 'moral'). Certainly, as Oakeshott himself observes, its subjection made the *universitas* a dubious model for a so-called 'free' or 'sovereign' state. But he could have added that the governing apparatus of the 'civil' state, consisting as it must of subordinate *personae* or offices, might thus be made answerable, as a legal person, to *lex*. Indeed, if we regard *lex* itself as a part, albeit a semi-autonomous part, of the state, and the state as a person, then it becomes possible for the subject (on whose assent *lex* in any case finally depends) to summon the state to his side in case of need, or even to hold it, paradoxical though it may seem, to its own laws.

This apparent weakness in a genuinely law-governed state is of course its real strength, and the source of its legitimacy. But in any state that merely affects to govern through law, though in fact governing by *diktaat*, it is a real, and perhaps its only, weakness (one, incidentally, that has been brilliantly exposed and exploited by the Czechoslovak dissident organisation, Charter 77). Where the state refuses to answer to its own would-be *lex*, it more or less openly concedes that law for it is a mere instrument of power or policy, and, in consequence, that the subject owes it no allegiance. That may make life no easier for the subject, but it makes it a lot more difficult for such a state, forced in this manner to divest itself of the last shred of any claim to authority. Indeed, if anything can be said to confirm the 'civil' state as (to borrow Aristotle's idiom) the 'true' or 'right' state, it is the constant attempt by 'perverted' collectivist teleocracies to pass themselves off as civil associations (*cf.* C 321 and n.).

The enterprise state

These speculations are much in Oakeshott's vein and wholly, I think, in his spirit. I can only suppose that his reluctance to push his own in a similar direction stems from his reluctance to recognise the state as, in its way, a genuine, morally responsible person or agent, since this might seem to concede the case for it as a *universitas*. Certainly on Oakeshott's showing most interpretations of the state as *universitas* exhibit a totalitarian or at least highly *dirigiste* tendency (C 263-313). These include: the state as the management, exploitation and development of an estate (whence the word 'state'); the state as an industrial enterprise; technocracy; the state as an administrative machine; the state as tutor or schoolmaster; the state as a salvationary, redemptive or therapeutic project; the state as a welfare agency and dispensary of benefits; in other words, the state as anything but a *civitas*, and its subjects not as *cives*, but as children, conscripts, invalids, dependents or just so much *matériel*.

Of course *dirigisme* is an intrinsic feature of enterprise association, and perfectly acceptable there, since enterprise association is by definition voluntary. What is wrong with the 'enterprise state' is that it cannot be a genuine enterprise association, since citizenship is compulsory. It is in fact a chimera or monstrosity: 'when a state is understood as a purposive association the analogy has been fatally corrupted: association in terms of a common substantive purpose must spring from the choice of each associate to be thus joined with others, a choice which he must be able to revoke' (C 319; *cf.* C 61 and R 45, 53).

It is one thing to be obliged to acknowledge the authority of *lex*; another (not far removed from slavery) to be forced to participate in unchosen substantive projects. The 'will' involved in the enterprise state is not that of the citizens or individuals concerned, nor yet that which T.H. Green distinguished from 'force' as the true 'basis of the state' (i.e. consent, embodied in *lex*), but the will of its 'managers'. If some subjects nevertheless identify their purposes with the state's, that means only that they too participate, for what they can get out of it, in the managerial tyranny exercised over their dissentient fellows. 'To the obedient,' Oakeshott says, 'will accrue a share in the profits of the enterprise ... The member of such a state enjoys the composure of the conscript assured of his dinner. His "freedom" is warm, compensated servility' (C 317).

Individuality and the state

As a concept, the enterprise state is almost as old as the civil state, and is not a specific response to modern conditions, though it has seemed to many to be particularly appropriate to them (and clearly socialism is one version of it). Its growing popularity since the 17th century, however, has been due neither to the so-called 'rise', nor to the social consequences, of capitalism. The 17th-century enterprise state was at once (as in Bacon's version) a political response to the new technological possibilities opened up by scientific discovery, and an ideological reaction to the growth of individuality. That - of which 'capitalism' was only one expression among many - was a propensity to detach oneself from communal anonymity, to enjoy making one's own decisions and to prize one's distinctness, which had arisen as early as the 12th century and, by the late Renaissance, bade fair to conquer Europe (*cf.* Burckhardt). Roughly for the same reasons as he earlier denied that 'self-enactment' was necessarily egoistic, Oakeshott is particularly sharp with those, Marxists and others, who would reduce this emergent moral self-understanding to an epiphenomenon of increasingly 'capitalist' economic arrangements. (He has, of course, C.B. Macpherson's so-called 'possessive individualism' in mind: see C 242n.)

The state as *universitas*, Oakeshott says, did not appeal to 'the poor' as such, though it did to those who saw them as an unexploited or under-used 'resource', as also to ambitious 'leaders' in search of a constituency. Indeed, he reminds us, one 17th-century democrat (he means Col. Rainborough of the Putney Debates, whom by a curious oversight he calls Buffcoat, which is what, not who, he was), actually claimed that the 'poorest he' was an 'individual' in the sense intended (C 241, 245); that is, should be counted fit for membership of a political *societas* simply in virtue of his manifest capacity for autonomy, of his having (if memory serves) 'a life to live, as much as the richest'.

'Poverty' and 'the masses'

Oakeshott has been taken to task for his supposed contempt, or lack of 'compassion', for 'the poor' (see, e.g. C 275f., 304f.). I do not believe that the relevant passages can sustain such a reading. Much depends on whom we take 'the poor' to signify (Oakeshott invariably puts them between quotation marks). It is true that he has expressed scepticism about (Roosevelt's) 'freedom from want' (R 39); true also that, while seemingly approving Hegel's proposals for industrial legislation and poor relief, he has objected that both 'force' (*viz*. life in the enterprise state) and 'eleemosynary benefits' emasculate the capacity for agency (in other words, keep 'the poor' dependent, and threaten everybody's freedom, their own included). But this objection surely embodies the genuine 'sympathy and respect' for them that according to Oakeshott only a few of their 'leaders' or spokesmen have ever felt. (He does not, however, mention Hegel's humane and persuasive arguments for public education of the poor, intended in part to elicit and reinforce their capacity for agency.)

Oakeshott's 'poor' posed a real political problem, but not because they were materially poor (they often were not). Their poverty was spiritual; it was not, for instance, found in the peasant, nor in the vagabond, nor invariably in the unpropertied 'proletarian'. It consisted, says Oakeshott, in their inability to meet the challenge of individuality, and their resulting loss of self-esteem in the face of its visible advance. Oakeshott is somewhat dismissive of 'alienation', perhaps because it usually implies a collectivist remedy (C 257, 279, 310, 321). Nevertheless, alienation is substantially what he portrays in the 'individual *manqué*' and (what his 'leaders' were determined to make of him) the 'anti-individual' or 'mass man', dedicated to the elimination of all that convicted him of inadequacy.

Oakeshott's comments on *ressentiment* in *On Human Conduct* are brief, alluding only by implication to the extended accounts given by Nietzsche, Dostoevsky, Scheler, and (in our own time) Schoeck. But unlike them, he is inclined to play down its significance. 'From one point of view,' he notes, '"the masses" must be regarded as the invention of their leaders', since their desires (except that of being relieved of the burden of choice) were not their own, but put into their mouths by their masters 'by a familiar trick of ventriloquism', *viz.* the plebiscite and the doctrine of the 'mandate' (M 161, 167; and *cf.* J1 474-5). Moreover, 'the desire of "the masses" to enjoy the products of individuality has modified their destructive urge' (one recalls Mr Wedgwood Benn's lofty disapproval of his council-house constituents' brass door-knockers). And, most heartening of all, the so-called 'mass man' shows 'an unquenchable propensity to desert at the call of individuality' (M 169). For this reason among others, perhaps, 'in the five centuries of modern European history ... the voice of civil association has, here and there, sunk to a whisper, but nowhere has it been totally silenced' (C 313).

The civil state

What, finally, will life be like in the 'civil' state, the state considered as *societas*, and why should anyone prize it?

We know, of course, that it will be united by a sentiment of 'civility'. But it will lack the hot, stifling intimacy of 'community' (for which Oakeshott, a true modernist in this respect, expresses little affection). It will not be held together by 'the morality of communal ties' (R 249-50/A 76-7). Indeed, though the city-state is one of its models, Oakeshott clearly envisages something far wider and more diverse. Too distant for love or hatred, relations in such a society will yet not be so distant as to exclude respect, nor (since all are protected by law) to exclude trust, a general presumption between strangers of each other's fair and friendly intent. The prevailing ethic will (within reason) be one of 'live and let live'.

It may be observed that, under such slogans as 'solidarity', 'fraternity', etc., the enterprise state invariably endeavours to recreate 'communal' sentiment at state level (where it becomes a 'morality of the common good': *ibid.*, and *cf.* C 324). Moreover, while local or personal ties may very occasionally be so strong as to inhibit a citizen's assent to *lex*, they are, like individuality, permanent obstacles to the all-embracing 'purpose' of the enterprise state, which will do everything it can to destroy them at source, honeycombing all subordinate associations with spies, and if necessary raising whole communities to the ground and dispersing or exterminating their populations.

Enterprise associations, of course, will flourish in the civil state. Their purposes do not conflict with the state's (as they do with the enterprise state's), since the state itself has no 'purpose'. Some, no doubt, will be unedifying; others simply daft ('there are those who spend their lives trying to sell copies of the Anglican Catechism to the Jews', R 184). And some will be economic, enriching their members by benefiting others. But prosperity and productivity, even though they may be expected to increase under the civil state, cannot be its direct concern. Qua state, it is not a 'free enterprise' but a 'no enterprise' state (C 318). (According to Oakeshott, maintaining a stable currency is almost its sole legitimate economic concern: R 58, 191.)

Freedom and autonomy

What all self-chosen activities testify to, be they transactional engagements, self-disclosures or self-enactments, is freedom. Oakeshott's view of freedom has some limited affinities with Mill's, but is both more subtle and more persuasive. First, freedom is a postulate of agency simply as such, because all conduct (even a slave's) is an 'intelligent' response to circumstances (C 36-7). Freedom is not 'unconstrained will', because circumstances are constraints, and conduct cannot appear independently of them. (Hence Oakeshott's scorn for the Rationalist's 'free mind', which indeed is will unconstrained by circumstance.) Nor is freedom, at this elementary level, identical with the 'self-direction' or 'autonomy' which civil association may be expected to foster. Autonomy develops, nevertheless, out of the inherent 'freedom' of agency.

What has to be learnt (for it does not just happen) is how to turn this 'unsought "freedom" of conduct' into a satisfaction in its own right (C 236). Oakeshott might appear to be commending the Californian fad for 'doing one's own thing', or (like some consumerist booby, or indeed a Friedmanite) simply celebrating 'choice' for its own sake, irrespective of what is chosen. But he is no more commending those than he is endorsing Hobbes's 'felicity', the continuous gratification of a ceaseless stream of velleities (see R 253-4/A 81), or advocating Mill's open-ended 'experiments in living'. At least, Oakeshott's position can be assimilated to Mill's only if, against the evidence, we imagine Mill's 'experiments' as being conducted under far more complex, rigorous and subtle constraints than any specified under the head of avoiding 'injury to others', a formula which begs as many questions as it answers.

Autonomy, for Oakeshott, is ultimately a virtue (C 238-9), the condition of 'virtuous self-enactment'. No doubt in its less developed forms it is egoistic, but then so, and not less damagingly, is the servility of the 'mass man', who, reckoning all risk and effort as a cost, is concerned only to receive his 'wished-for satisfactions' at the hand of *soi-disant* authority. Even in the superficially self-directed man, egoism (as we have seen) is a kind of servitude, since where it prevails, his entire self-conception, and not merely his transitory elation or disappointment, must hinge on the fate of his substantive projects.

At its highest, Oakeshott's 'freedom' or 'individuality' has no such flaw. It is both the condition and the product of civil association. Presupposing a graceful acceptance of obligations, it consists in endeavouring to meet them in the most creative and appropriate way. Unlike the 'natural' freedom postulated by most thinkers in the liberal tradition (including Locke, and even in certain respects Mill), it can only be learnt and enjoyed in society, which can flourish only under its complement, law. It will be inhibited in the enterprise state, of course, by the absence of positive rights and the plethora of compulsory observances. In itself, however, Oakeshott's 'freedom' is not so much a right, still less a 'natural' right, as an individual and collective accomplishment. The moral character involved, Oakeshott says, is 'autonomous on account of its self-understanding and its command of resources it has made its own'. And, he adds, 'the half of this self-understanding is knowing its own limits' (C 237). The free man is not a lawless pirate, a neurotic rebel, or a banal self-seeker, but a virtuous explorer reckless (in the end) of worldly advantage, a model citizen - if any such could be prescribed - of the *civitas peregrina*, an association not of pilgrims but of adventurers (C 243).

7. The Modes (III): History and Poetry

Oakeshott's views on history have achieved a certain canonical status, and have been widely discussed. I know, however, of no systematic discussion of his aesthetics. Oakeshott himself has expended only 50 pages on them, as against over 200 on history. The aesthetic, nevertheless, is a category which permeates nearly all of his thought.

Reviewing *Experience and its Modes* Collingwood rightly remarked that it contained 'the most penetrating analysis of historical thought that has ever been written' (a view later repeated in his *The Idea of History*). No attentive reader can come away from the section on history in *Experience and its Modes* unimpressed by the ferocious critical brio with which, pillar by pillar, the young Oakeshott demolishes the conventional wisdom. Nor, on a more positive note, can one fail to be struck by the painstaking exactitude with which in *On History*, fifty years later, the old philosopher consolidates his position. Historiography is the only topic on which Oakeshott seems never to have shifted his ground.

As one might expect, the essence of his position throughout is a rejection of all realist, Rationalist, positivist, transcendental or reductionist views of history. History, or 'the historical past' (E 109, R 153, H 33-5, etc.), is a self-subsistent world created by the historian out of the available evidence (E 100, 109-12, 139). It is not an independent realm of 'fact'. Oakeshott does not deny that 'truth' in one sense is a quality of propositions, which possess it to the extent that they correspond with the things they describe (R 229). But if anything could make the Idealist 'coherence theory of truth' plausible it is surely history. There can be no 'correspondence' between events and the historian's account of them (E 93, 95, 108, 113), since it is precisely his job to establish what they were. They are simply 'what the evidence obliges us to believe': the conclusion, not the premise, of his reasonings (E 99, 125). Writing history, Oakeshott notes provocatively, is 'the only way of making it' (E 99; *cf.* H 33), and consists of nothing but making sense of the evidence, i.e. making it cohere.

It follows that to the historian (as to the Idealist) nothing can be irrelevant: 'every historical event is necessary'; 'nothing is excluded or regarded as "non-contributory"'; there is no place in history for 'the abnormal or the improbable' (E 129, 142; R 154; H 116). Oakeshott's historical 'necessity' is quite different from (e.g.) the Marxist's. For the Marxist, 'history', though unconscious, is effectively an agent. Like God for the Jews, Providence for St Augustine, 'the stars' for Burton, Great Men (one might add) for Carlyle, and 'will' or 'psychology' for various of their successors, it explains everything (E 103-4, 126-30). But that is merely to say that for the historian, like all such transcendent 'causes', it explains nothing. *'Pour savoir les choses, it faut savoir le détail'* (E 143).

Moreover, Oakeshott's conception rules out not only determinism, but also its opposite, 'chance' (see Chapter 6 above, on Bury). 'Chance' and 'accident', like 'intervention', and indeed like moral judgments, are practical, agent-relative considerations which history ultimately cannot recognise. As far as Charles V's policy was concerned, Oakeshott says, the Pope certainly did intervene; but for the historian it is meaningless to say (as one normally would) that his intervention 'changed the course of events', since (like William the Conqueror's 'accidental' death) it actually was the course of events (R 154). The Pope intervened, not in some notional alternative course of events, but only in (what their author hoped would be that course of events) Charles V's plans.

Oakeshott's general point here is clear and compelling. Nevertheless it seems as if his rigour had, in one respect, got the better of him. Charles V's plans certainly belonged to his practical present. But it is not obvious that they thereby belong to our practical past, and as such are irrelevant to history proper. Surely to treat the engagements and aspirations of past agents as practical for the agents concerned is not of itself to re-enter the practical mode. Oakeshott perhaps concedes as much in saying that while moral judgment of past actions is 'practical', and thus historically irrelevant, history does not exclude the description of conduct 'in, generally speaking, moral terms' (R 162-3).

Practical judgments on the past are not illegitimate; they are merely not historical. The 'practical past' consists of past events so far as they bear on present or subsequent interests. They are thus selected, edited, mythologised or otherwise abstracted from their context to suit. The practical man (like the 'Whig historian') reads history backwards: for him the past is a compendium of lessons, exempla, anticipations, warnings and inspirations, a storehouse of statecraft and practical wisdom (E 105, 157; R 153-4). Oakeshott does not deny its usefulness, still less its real existence as a present world. It amounts, in fact, to tradition (if also, in its more distorted forms, to ideology); and as what he calls 'quasi-history' it is of the greatest value to both the practitioner and the theorist of politics (R 130). Hence Oakeshott himself is not above recourse to it in support of his own political contentions. He does deny, however, that such a past is the past with which the historian proper is concerned.

To construe an event as an 'origin' is to characterise it in terms of its consequences, which obviously could not have been inherent in it. An event can only be understood retrospectively, in terms of its own past. Hence in history there are no 'origins', only 'noteworthy' or 'significant' antecedents (E 131; R 153, 160; H 64, 83, 88). Being separated from their consequences by no temporal interval (H 85), they are literally 'contingent' (see Chapter 6 above). Nothing in history works from outside or wholly at a distance; no event is 'latent' in its antecedents; there is no unfolding immanent pattern, no teleology, no Aristotelian 'final cause'. An historical 'cause', for Oakeshott, is a mere *façon de parler,* and explicitly has nothing to do with mechanism, determinism, or quasi-scientific 'laws'. It is always either direct or 'mediated' through other events (E 143, H 71).

These, indeed, may attenuate its character as a 'significant antecedent'. For example, if event A bears on event B, B on C, and so on up to G, it is clear that G, though (as Oakeshott would say) 'intelligibly' or 'contingently' related to A through events B to F, might (considered in isolation) retain no perceptible imprint of A whatever. Its relationship to A would be explicable solely in terms of the series B to F. 'The relation between events,' says Oakeshott, 'is always other events; and it is established in history by a full relation of the events'; 'the only explanation of change relevant or possible in history is simply a complete account of change' (E 143). What the historian does is simply, in the light of his evidence, to exhibit established 'subsequents' as plausible 'consequents' (H 72).

The relation between performances, as we have seen, is also one of 'contingency'. Nevertheless, history is not a mere record of performances or *res gestae* (H 34, 48, 51). It is a past which, unlike the performances from which it is inferred, 'has not itself survived' (H 33, 92). To infer it is not simply to reconstruct 'what must have happened', still less (H 56) to 'fill the gaps' by retrodicting unrecorded performances (as, e.g. Lucien Goldmann did in *Le Dieu Caché*). The historian's view is not a re-enactment or an imaginary eyewitness account (E 140, R 164). It cannot be a Collingwood-style 'living past' (R 166, H 18), for the following reasons.

First, unless it goes beyond the original participants' perspective, it will remain sunk in practice (most of their surviving utterances being in that idiom), and especially so if it confines itself to, or worse still adopts, the perspective of only some among the participants. These are crimes of which, under the metaphors of 'going native' and 'replacing sympathy by total immersion', Oakeshott convicts E.H. Carr (J4 344f.).

Secondly, the historian must inevitably postulate connections of which, though real enough, the original participants could never have been aware. Writing history, Oakeshott says, is 'the art of understanding men and events more profoundly than they were understood when they lived and happened' (*ibid*.). Hence the historical past not only did not survive, but 'could not have survived' (H 92). (Of course by 'more profoundly' Oakeshott implies no recourse to teleological or consequential explanations; he means only 'more completely'.)

And thirdly, historical events, unlike mere actions or 'exploits', are not 'assignable performances' (H 33, 49, 64). An historical 'event' is literally the outcome (*eventus*) of multifarious and often otherwise unrelated 'occurrences', as those are of similarly divergent performances. It cannot be finally explained in terms of intentions, not because the performances involved were unintentional (they were not), but because in general (and as Tolstoy constantly observes in *War and Peace*) it will not specifically have been intended or prefigured in them. Oakeshott gives no example, but an obvious analogy would be the movement of a market independently of the buyers' and sellers' intentions, of which it is nevertheless wholly the result. (On the other hand, he seems firmly disposed not to treat history as one of the social sciences, which, as noted in Chapter 6 above, are to a great extent the study of unintended consequences.)

In all these respects the historical past is not what it was for the agents concerned, a 'living past', but a dead. And as for the historical 'individual' (that is, any intelligible object of study), its identity is neither imposed from without, nor incapable of being redrawn in the light of criticism or fresh evidence, but consists simply in whatever coherence the historian, working to his chosen scale, manages to elicit from his material (R 166-7; H 114). Its limits are simply the limits of coherence. Beyond them, either the designated 'individual' changes out of all recognition (i.e. ceases to exist), or (one might add) the evidence simply becomes too scanty for the principle of contingency to operate.

Oakeshott's conception of history and historiography may be a 'severe and sophisticated manner of thinking about the world' (R 166), but it is not so rarefied as to be impossible of realization. Indeed, his is essentially an attempt to make explicit the principles of the historiography which was emerging in his youth into an eminence it has not yet lost. Then, it was thought, history had finally emancipated itself from Practice (typified especially by religion and 'retrospective politics') and in that sense, if in no other, was entitled to dignify itself with the label 'scientific'.

Few history books, of course, will ever consist solely of Oakeshottian history, and in that respect (like civil association) his 'history' is an 'ideal type'. That, however, does not affect his outstanding achievement, which is to have whittled down to its differentia a highly various practice, represented by historians as diverse as Tocqueville and Maitland, by political history and *mentalité* alike, and by perspectives ranging from the wafer-thin time-slices and ultra-parochial settings of some of the Annales school to the *longues durées* and vast geographical panoramas of others such as Braudel. No-one who has pondered Oakeshott will ever again be able to see (e.g.) that standard freshman authority, E.H. Carr's *What Is History?*, as anything much more than a stream of well-meaning howlers.

In 'The Voice of Poetry in the Conversation of Mankind', Oakeshott similarly attempts to whittle down aesthetic experience to its differentia, but to my mind the result is less convincing. It also testifies, unlike his historical writings, to a remarkable volte-face.

'The Voice of Poetry', Oakeshott tells us, is 'a belated retraction of a foolish sentence in *Experience and its Modes*' (R, preface). The sentence in question I take to be this: 'For in these [*sc*. ''art, music and poetry''], in the end, we are wholly taken up with practical life' (E 297). A few years later Oakeshott wrote in similar vein that 'the genius of the poet and artist and to a lesser extent of the philosopher is to create and recreate the values of their society' (P 150).

These contentions certainly need qualification, but they do not seem altogether foolish. The claim that art has some bearing on Practice, especially in point of possessing a moral dimension (something that Oakeshott is later at great pains to deny), belongs, if not to a dominant, at least to a respectable critical tradition. But if art is 'in the end' wholly practical, what becomes of the crucial (and, one would have thought, quintessentially modal) distinction between fiction and 'reality'? If there is none, then Partridge's innocent credulity at Garrick's Hamlet in Tom Jones, or people's sending wreaths to television companies on the 'deaths' of their favourite soap opera characters, would seem entirely rational. Oakeshott gives similar examples in 'The Voice of Poetry' (R 226) to justify his new position, to the effect that art, after all, has nothing whatever to do with Practice.

Like history, and simply as a matter of fact, works of art, even if originally 'practical' (magical, devotional, didactic, etc.), have increasingly become what science always was, an 'escape' or emancipation from Practice (R 238, 242). Oakeshott is actually referring to a change in our habits of artistic appreciation, which is such that historic works (e.g. Russian icons) have lost their original meanings and acquired others; but of course the same change is perceptible in artistic creation too. That is not to say that art is 'escapist', merely that the aesthetic has achieved modal autonomy, and is thus valuable in its own right. 'Poetry', as Oakeshott calls the aesthetic generically, consists in 'images' which, since they refer to no 'outside' world, are entirely (and surprisingly) non-symbolic (R 224-5).

Poetry's sole end is 'delight', *viz.* the enjoyment of these images for their own sake. Anything (in principle) may be viewed 'poetically', not only art, but also natural and found objects; and our response to those, involving as it does the deliberate suspension of desire and other 'practical' impulses (Kant's aesthetic 'disinterestedness'), is equally with art a kind of creative poesis. (Thus once again the distinction between fiction and reality disappears, for all is now effectively fiction, being essentially a matter of how we, the spectators, elect to view things.) Poetry, then, is pure 'contemplation', a unique and wholly self-enclosed activity, divorced at once from Practice and (like conversation, but unlike science and history) from argument and inquiry; for those are analogues, perhaps even residues, of the purposiveness inherent in Practice.

It is hard to know precisely what to make of these contentions. Somewhere, undoubtedly, among the phenomena usually recognised as aesthetic, there exists a peculiarly pure and self-sufficient 'delight', such as one might experience in contemplating a flower, a sea-shell, or a Japanese pot. It is found even in literature, which, sharing as it does much of its vocabulary with practice, is generally hard to strip of its practical resonances. And it may well be that an art-work, like any other object, in which this 'delight' is nowhere to be found cannot qualify, even in everyday, non-Oakeshottian terms, as 'poetic'. In other words, whatever admixture, or indeed preponderance, of moral, satirical, representational, documentary or other elements a given art-work may contain, if it does not also induce 'delight' it is not a (real? successful?) work of art. Conversely, some works of art may consist of little or nothing else than expressly 'delightful' images. Virginia Woolf (whom Oakeshott greatly admires) detected some such aesthetic purity in Elizabethan literature; and some, certainly, might claim that it is found also in her own.

I have earlier discounted any substantial affiliation between Oakeshott and Bloomsbury, but, one might say, here it is after all, in his apparent 'aestheticism'. Have we not in 'The Voice of Poetry' something like the amoral formalism of Roger Fry and Clive Bell, and before them Pater, Whistler and Wilde? It might seem so, were it not for the fact that the aesthetic, as Oakeshott now conceives of it, has absorbed into itself so many moral and religious phenomena of the 'higher' kind. And it should be said straight away that those phenomena, in thus migrating to the aesthetic sphere from the practical (which has accordingly become more exclusively utilitarian or prudential), have abated nothing of their ethically admirable character. Oakeshott is emphatically not one for whom the spectacle of goodness provides merely a delicious *frisson*. So far from having aestheticised (and thus denatured) the moral, in fact, he has partially moralised the aesthetic, even if in so doing he has made less credible his purely 'aesthetic' conception of what Poetry is.

Love, friendship, and moral goodness, we are told, all contain intimations of 'poetry' (R 244-5), just as later, in *On Human Conduct*, 'virtue', along with 'self-enactment' generally, is said to have an aesthetic dimension. Like religion in *On Human Conduct*, moral goodness is characterised, in the very same words, as a release from 'the deadliness of doing', i.e. from Practice narrowly conceived (R 245, C 74). In 'The Voice of Poetry' a May morning is a 'poetic image'; in *On Human Conduct* it is religious, 'an encounter with eternity' (R 229-30, C 85). (It should be added that 'religion' in *On Human Conduct* is more like a numinous awareness or simple piety, and thus an 'escape' from all the normal assertive, dogmatic, and purposive aspects of religion, which by implication remain firmly fixed in Practice. This of course is a very post-Romantic, 'demythologizing' view.)

Whether love, friendship and the rest are now fully 'poetic', or merely, as Oakeshott says, 'a connection between the voices of poetry and practice, a channel of common understanding' (R 244), i.e. still ambiguously practical, is of little consequence, except to Oakeshott's modal theory. What matters here is whether it is plausible to regard the moral considerabilities they embody as irrelevant to fiction. If they have at least a foothold in Poetry generally, and are thus a source of 'delight', why should they be excluded, as Oakeshott excludes them, specifically from art? One is reminded of Nabokov's postcript to *Lolita*, in which, having just identified his aim as 'aesthetic bliss', he then lists the unexceptionable moral sentiments ('curiosity, kindness, tenderness, ecstasy') in which it consists.

Oakeshott seems reluctant to admit that 'real-life' emotions and judgments can carry over into art. We are 'held back', he says, 'from approving or disapproving' of 'Anna Karenina, Lord Jim, or the Duchess Sanseverina', on account of 'their unmistakably poetic quality' (R 227). All that this really testifies to (and it is, I think, false) is that, because we know them to be fictions, we do not literally approve or disapprove (etc.) of them. But it is surely wrong to imply that in contemplating fictional characters or situations, and when the particular work seems to indicate (and justify) such a response, we do not experience, or internally rehearse, emotions and attitudes at least akin to those appropriate to the equivalent 'real' events. The 'pity' and 'terror' of tragedy (Aristotle) do not of course lead us actually to rush on stage to condole with the sufferers, or to flee the theatre in anticipation of the catastrophe; but the spectator who, fully aware that the events before him are imaginary, nevertheless weeps at Cordelia's forgiveness of her father, or at Lear's entrance with her dead in his arms, is neither the subject of a purely 'aesthetic' emotion (though there is certainly one involved somewhere) nor the victim of a category-mistake. And the same surely holds in the more complex case of moral judgments.

It may be said that, at best, Oakeshott has identified the differentia of art, *viz.* that it is fiction. (But as we have seen, so also in its way is any object of 'contemplation'.) We are surely not required, however, to accept that morality, religion, etc., once they too achieve 'poetic' status, somehow become less 'real'. Nor can we suppose that a work of art subsists purely in its delight-inducing properties (which it may share with non-fictional objects), or that these are readily separable from the representational or quasi-practical 'images' in which they are embedded. (To suppose so might be like the Rationalist's belief in pure 'intelligence'.)

The examples Oakeshott gives of the 'unpoetic' in art - Hardy's pessimism, Chopin's patriotism, Dante's theology, Ingres' verisimilitude (R 243) - are not only ill-assorted but unconvincing too, for almost any could, at will, be taken as an object for 'contemplation' and thus become a source of 'delight', without altogether giving up whatever 'serious' meaning it had for its author. Oakeshott would have done well to reconsider the view, which he dismisses somewhat too readily, of art (or at least of some art) as 'make-believe' (R 207, 227, 239). For it accounts not only for the ability of situations recognised as fictional to evoke 'real' emotions - what Marianne Moore meant by calling poetry 'an imaginary garden with real toads in it' - but also for our ability to sympathise, where appropriate, with an author's beliefs and purposes without actually sharing them (an intensified version, perhaps, of Dilthey's and Weber's *Verstehen*).

Oakeshott, however, is little disposed to make any concessions to so-called 'author's meaning', except when, as he occasionally does, he cites a literary work in support of some non-literary contention (e.g. *Anna Karenina* on the folly of Rationalism, R 96n.; *cf.* R 23n., 31n.). This follows from his beliefs, first, that aesthetic experience is *sui generis*, and therefore cannot 'refer' outside itself, or consequently 'mean' anything; and second, that it is essentially generated not by the object (a work of art or nature) but by the subject (i.e. the reader, spectator, 'contemplator', etc.). Moreover, as we have seen earlier, such a subject-centred aesthetic more or less abolishes the distinction between art and nature, which is marked solely by the presence or absence of intention, and it is intention alone, as with any utterance, which gives credibility to the idea of an author's meaning. There are elements in Oakeshott's aesthetics which bring him close, in certain respects, to the *Nouvelle Critique* of such as Barthes and Derrida, though not, be it said, to their modishness, pretentiousness, obscurantism and general intellectual confusion, which until very recently bade fair to conquer every university literature department in the Western world.

For Oakeshott, in the end, Poetry remains ambiguous, paradoxical and plural. It is ultimately not divorced from 'the values of society' precisely because, as with conversation and liberal education, its autonomy, its ability to liberate us more completely even than Science and History from 'the deadliness of doing', itself constitutes a 'value'. (Like those, it is a component of Aristotle's 'leisure' or *scholè*, the true, if non-practical, 'purpose' of human life: cf. R 221.) Oakeshott admits as much in commending Schiller's views on the 'social value' of art, and his 'thoughts on the usefulness of a "useless" activity' (play). And he abandons almost all of his aestheticism - not to say his whole case - in observing that Shelley's claim, to the effect that 'poets are the unacknowledged legislators of the world', may after all be 'merely a reflection of the manifold character of Apollo' (R 240-1).

8. Oakeshott and Contemporary Thought

'We don't feel very securely at home,' wrote Rilke in his first *Duino Elegy*, 'in this interpreted world.' But for Oakeshott, as for Grote, we should, first because (as Rilke eventually concluded) it is 'our' world, in that we have made it, and secondly because there is no other. 'To be human and to be aware,' says Oakeshott at the beginning of *On Human Conduct*, 'is to encounter only what is in some manner understood ... we inexorably inhabit a world of intelligibles.'

The general recognition of Wittgenstein's importance has already paved the way, especially in America, for a positive reassessment of Oakeshott (see, e.g., Richard Rorty's *Philosophy and the Mirror of Nature*, where Oakeshott is found rubbing shoulders not only with Wittgenstein but, for reasons just touched on above, with assorted post-structuralists too). Wittgenstein's so-called 'idealism' may be sufficiently illustrated here by a handful of well-known *dicta*: 'what has to be accepted, the given, is forms of life'; 'what is hidden, for example, can be of no interest to us'; 'don't look for the meaning, look for the use'; 'philosophy leaves everything as it is'. What they have in common lies also at the centre of Oakeshott's thought, *viz.* a rejection of any noumenal, transcendental, naturalistic or (so to speak) Archimedean standpoint outside experience from which to judge or correct it.

What is rejected, in essence, is the great modernist and Rationalist illusion (sedulously fostered by Marx and Freud, and exploited by a host of charlatans) of 'depth'. Oakeshott and Wittgenstein, by contrast, reaffirm what Roger Scruton has called 'the priority of appearance': the idea that things are, on the whole, what they appear to be and articulate themselves, in no matter how complex a fashion, intelligibly enough on the surface to demand explanation, at least at the outset, in appropriately 'superficial' terms. It may thus be plausible, as John Gray has suggested, to see Oakeshott even as a post-modernist.

For both Oakeshott and Wittgenstein (as for Rilke) experience is ultimately not given but made. To be sure, it is 'given' in language; but language is a social artefact, the tangible deposit of a 'form of life', just as, in turn, a 'form of life' could not subsist without the public concepts embodied in language. Moreover, the Wittgensteinian notion of separate 'language-games' governed solely by their internal rules and conventions has something in common, not only with Oakeshott's modes, but also with his idea that the *geistige Welt* (like the civil association which sustains it) is similarly self-sufficient.

It is tempting to assimilate Oakeshott's sociological 'conservatism' to that of Wittgensteinians such as Peter Winch. For Winch, certainly, as for Oakeshott, 'a belief is what it means to the believer' (C 23, 36; *cf.* V 64). Winch is inclined, accordingly, to justify as rational any coherent, non-falsifiable world-view such as that of the East African Azande people (documented by the anthropologist E.E. Evans-Pritchard in his 1936 classic, *Witchcraft, Oracles and Magic Among the Azande*).

It is not clear, however, how far Oakeshott would agree. The facts that a belief *a fortiori* must 'make sense' to the believer, and that he is able to explain, or explain away, whatever appears to confute it, do not, of themselves, make it 'true'. For these, after all, are characteristic less of the unselfconscious practices and traditions which Oakeshott celebrates (and which the Marxist would call 'ideology') than of ideologies in the Oakeshottian sense (the sense in which Marxism is an ideology). Traditions, for Oakeshott, possess an inventiveness, adaptability, and capacity for self-criticism that is found neither in Rationalism nor in 'primitive' world-views such as that of the Azande; Oakeshott, indeed, has stigmatised Rationalism as 'the relic of a belief in magic' (R 92; *cf.* R 22, 122). We have seen also that, in Oakeshott's opinion, the beliefs of historical agents cannot fully explain the events to which those agents contributed. And finally, the modes, though self-subsistent in point of their comparative internal coherence, are not in any absolute sense 'real'. All these considerations must seriously qualify any attempt to see Oakeshott as a full-blooded Winchian organicist or (sociological) functionalist.

At the same time, Oakeshott is by no means a straightforward Popperian. Popper's falsifiability-criterion (the idea that no proposition can be scientifically 'true' which is not open to possible empirical refutation) implicitly assumes a correspondence theory of truth, which Oakeshott either rejects or implicitly includes within a wider coherence theory. Thus the correspondence theory is useless in history (see Chapter 7 above), but would presumably hold in science in virtue of the fact that non-correspondence between theory and observation is a species of incoherence. (Theory, moreover, is internal to science.) It is clear also that Oakeshott must reject Popper's 'methodological individualism' - the belief that human activity must ultimately be understood in terms of the psychology of individuals - since the individual and his 'psychology' are inseparable from, or at least not independent of, their social relations and their social inheritance. Thus far, at any rate, Oakeshott is an organicist: *cf.* his dictum that 'everything figures, not with what stands next to it, but with the whole' (R 128, 134).

Nevertheless, as political thinkers Oakeshott and Popper belong to the same post-war anti-Rationalist, anti-totalitarian tendency, even despite Popper's commendation of what might be called small-scale Rationalism, *viz.* 'piecemeal engineering'. Popper's awareness of the open-ended, unpredictable growth of knowledge, and Oakeshott's of the similar open-enedness of all practices, lead them both to oppose the Rationalist's pretensions to absolute, definitive, quasi-scientific *gnosis*. Both, indeed, have something in common with Wittgenstein's cousin Hayek (as they also do with Polanyi).

For Hayek human needs are perceptible to no central observer, and hence to no government. Rather, knowledge of them is horizontally dispersed throughout the myriad voluntary transactions between individuals in a free society (an idea which goes back at least to Burke's *Thoughts and Details on Scarcity*). For Oakeshott this dispersal is also vertical and diachronic. The needful is embodied not only in whatever satisfactions the market, or transactional engagement generally, can deliver, but more especially in tradition and common law. These transcend economic or even narrowly political considerations, having a moral and cultural dimension generally absent from Hayek's thought.

Of late, however, Hayek has moved perceptibly in an Oakeshottian direction, with his critique of socialism and the like as being an expression, paradoxically, of individualistic *hubris* (*The Fatal Conceit* is a recent title). Such doctrines involve the belief (which Hayek calls 'constructivist rationalism') that the individual, by using his own reasoning powers, can provide general 'solutions' to others' specific 'problems'. Genuine rationality in social matters, as for Oakeshott, is collective, though not in the sense of residing in formal collective decisions, rather in emerging spontaneously, on the model of Adam Smith's 'invisible hand' (or even, perhaps, of Oakeshott's 'conversation'), from the aggregate nexus of decisions agreed between individuals negotiating under a common framework of laws and conventions. (Thus unintended consequences may be by no means undesired or undesirable.)

For all that, Oakeshott's purview is much wider than either Popper's or Hayek's; unlike them he endeavours to give a complete account of human experience. He is, in fact, much more fully a philosopher, and even his political philosophy is only a part of the whole. It is perhaps for this reason, which goes along with his relative lack of interest in day-to-day politics and his consequent reluctance to offer any detailed policy prescriptions, that he has suffered comparative public neglect.

I have already suggested that Oakeshott cannot be assimilated to those leading figures in the so-called 'revival' of political philosophy, Rawls and Nozick. This is not because he is more conservative, nor because where liberal he is so in neither of their opposed fashions (left-liberal and libertarian respectively). It is because he is far less abstract and far more historically-minded. Unlike

Oakeshott, neither Rawls nor Nozick connects with, or even attempts to describe, the moral and political intuitions of the ordinary citizen. Rawls addresses himself, in the Kantian manner, simply to all rational beings independent of any civil or social order (and hence without any conception of an end beyond themselves, or even of themselves as possessing any determinate content), with a view to their choosing one 'from outside'. Nozick, on the other hand, bases his argument on confessedly dogmatic Lockean 'rights' pertaining to a notional pre-political, or even pre-social, 'individual'. Both of them, however, echo the concerns of the modern politician. Those have become what H.D. Lasswell once gratingly described as the central concern of political philosophy, *viz.* 'who gets what, when and how.' If that is really what political philosophy is all about, then not only is it excruciatingly banal, but its 'revival' is also thoroughly Rationalist.

There also seems little to link Oakeshott with the two grand old men of American conservatism, the German scholars Strauss and Voegelin. Oakeshott favourably reviewed Strauss on Hobbes in 1937 (A 132f.), and later had kind words for Voegelin. He has subsequently said, however, that he finds Strauss 'naïve'. Doubtless he had in mind Strauss's habit of de-historicising his subjects, so that thinkers from antiquity to the present are really 'talking heads' conducting a single argument across the centuries in search of perennial truth. It is hard also to see how Oakeshott could accept Strauss's invariable antithesis between an author's 'exoteric' and 'esoteric' doctrines, since it leaves the reader at complete liberty, if it fits his theory, to interpret what is being said as meaning precisely the opposite. This is unfalsifiability with a vengeance.

Nor can I see how, given his historical relativism, Oakeshott could regard as useful Voegelin's immensely long trawl, through a Toynbee-like panorama of civilisations from Sumer and Ancient Egypt onwards, for the Platonic Good (*cf.* Strauss's perennial truth). Voegelin does, however, stress that the Good as such can never be the direct concern of politics. To attempt to realize it in the political sphere, is to fall into the vice of 'gnosticism', which is a secular substitute for religion and closely resembles Oakeshott's Rationalism. In this, certainly, we may expect Oakeshott to concur. But it seems unlikely, considering what Oakeshott has said about Royalism, Anglicanism, and 'ideological' conservatism generally (see Chapter 4 above), and the somewhat dim view he takes of 'community' (see Chapter 6), that he would regard Voegelin's concept of 'existential representation' - the visible, quasi-mystical symbolization of a people's political identity in a person or institution - as either necessary or very significant. It seems, in sum, that even Strauss and Voegelin may be too 'rationalist' for his taste.

I have already noted that the 'darker' side of politics is under-represented in Oakeshott. In part this may be merely a reflection of his personal disposition, which, though by no means without its serious side, nor unqualified by the experience of war, is both warmly affectionate and coolly optimistic. Oakeshott is certainly the least inclined among moralists and political thinkers to go in for adolescent or crisis-mongering. (Consider, for example, his refreshingly level-headed reflections on The Bomb: V 108-10.)

The politics of crisis, for Oakeshott, are both the product of an overheated Rationalist imagination and its natural, all-too-real consequence in practice (R 3, 5, 23, 31, 35; *cf.* C 64). He would hardly deny, however, the importance of, say, class-conflicts or power-struggles in politics (see, e.g., 'The Political Economy of Freedom', R 37f.). But he would also be the last to make them fundamental: first, because the quest for foundations is quintessentially Rationalist; secondly, because membership of a class, at least of a class qua political agency, is not, as the Marxist would claim, wholly 'objectively' determined. Socially conditioned it may be, but it is also a matter of one's self-conception or subjective allegiance, and must become more so the less pressing economic considerations become.

On one thing, however, Marx and Oakeshott are agreed, *viz.* that theory is the shadow of practice. For Marx all thought (his own being a notable example) derives from Practice in Oakeshott's narrowest, most teleocratic and egoistic conception of it. For Oakeshott, by contrast, each practice (of which Practice is only one, and by no means the most estimable or most definitively human) generates its own appropriate universe of thought.

From what practice or manifold of practices, it may finally be asked, does Oakeshott's own thought then derive, and does this not qualify its claim to be taken seriously? The two questions may be answered together: it derives from a tradition of freedom and pluralism, and precisely for that reason, because (though conditional) it is not compelled but chosen, it deserves to be treated with respect, on its own terms. Characterising his and his readers' political heritage, Oakeshott wrote that:

> Our need now is to recover the lost sense of a society whose freedom and organization spring, not from a superimposed plan, but from the integrating power of a vast and subtle body of rights and duties enjoyed between individuals (whose individuality, in fact, comes into being by their enjoyment), not the gift of nature but the product of our own experience and inventiveness; and to recover also the perception of our law, not merely as a body of achieved rights and duties, the body of a freedom in which mere political rights have a comparatively insignificant place, but as a living method of social integration, the most civilized and the most effective method ever invented by mankind. (J1 490)

Those words were written in 1948, which may excuse the whiff of restorationist sentiment they contain. But they are not less relevant in our controversial times. For what they point to is a 'form of life' in which 'mere' politics, along with Practice, is kept severely in its place.

The same goes, in the end, for philosophy. To philosophise, Oakeshott wrote, is necessarily 'to surrender the green for the grey' (E 3). Yet, he concluded, 'there is perhaps something decadent, even depraved, in the attempt to achieve a completely coherent world of experience' (E 356). Hegel too had argued for the priority of 'forms of life' over their own explanations: 'when philosophy paints its grey in grey, then has a shape of life grown old.' Both Oakeshott and

Hegel are tacitly alluding to Mephistopheles' famous words to the student in Goethe's Faust. They make an admirable epigraph to Oakeshott's work:

Grau, theurer Freund, ist alle Theorie,
Und grün des Lebens goldner Baum.

'Grey, dear friend, is all theory, and green the golden tree of life'. The theory which tells us so, however (and as I hope I have shown), is not grey, but green . Not only does it begin from life, but it also returns us to it, both wiser and more appreciative of life's charm, variety and worth.

Appendix: Oakeshott on his Schooldays

To me [St George's] was a world of remarkable personalities, each very different from the others ... But [Grant] was the centre of it, and although more remote than the other human components, the greatest single influence upon me. ... The virtue of some schoolmasters is that they remain 'boys at heart'; the virtue of Grant was that he was unmistakably an adult. ...

[He did not] seem to generate immediate affection; at all events he did not rule by the affection he generated ... The loyalty he provoked was very much a loyalty to the community. ...

I do not think that a sheer love of learning was by any means his first love, but I think it was this, among other other things, [that] he imparted to me. ...

His power of creating a myth, a legend, was quite remarkable. ... For a community of so short a duration it was remarkably equipped with heroes, with a past and a relationship to that past - a relationship which sometimes seemed to stretch back to the early Christians. ... Think of the romantic haze he spread over the Dottoressa [Montessori] ...

Religion did not appear as a set of beliefs but as a kind of *pietas*; morals was knowing how to behave; Florentine and Pre-Raphaelite art was on the walls. These things were very little 'intellectualised', and afterwards, when some of them were left behind, I never felt that they were things I had to be released from. ...

For a man with great force of personality and immense skill in imparting it, Grant was remarkably 'undominating'. ... It was a style of life, rather than a doctrine, he imparted. ...

I did value very greatly the association we had with girls, but I don't think that co-education has any detectable influence in making 'the relations of the sexes' better, whatever that may mean. ...

The happiness was a kind of serenity; growing up was something to be enjoyed, not merely got through ... I don't ever remember being bored .... What St George's provided ... was a feeling of safety and an immense variety of outlets ... Some of my schooldays were abnormal, even for St George's, because of the war ...; from that point of view [of learning what one is expected to learn at school] they were highly inefficient. ... I do not think that my happiness depended upon being allowed the immense amount of freedom we were allowed - or what it really was at times, being neglected and allowed to roam. It did depend, however, on the huge range of quite informal opportunities. St George's was a place surrounded by a thick, firm hedge, and inside this hedge was a world of beckoning activities and interests. Many of them emanated from Grant himself, many of them were the private enterprise of members of staff, some one made for oneself. There was a great deal of laughter and fun; there was a great deal of seriousness. ...

I think Grant's intention was to centre himself pretty firmly in the sort of grammar school education which had been knocking around England for centuries and from which the Victorian public schools emerged, and to innovate on this tradition in certain specific directions. Some of these innovations were designed to mitigate specific evils; many belonged to the wave of enterprise in the early years of this century which threw up a vast number of 'experimental' schools. I don't think I should regard Grant as essentially an 'experimentalist' - his convictions were far too firm to allow him to start something just to see what happened. But for a man of such convictions he was extraordinarily unfussy; and he separated himself easily from educational cranks.

(From *St George's School, 1907-1967: a Portrait of the Founders*, ed. H.W. Howe, Harpenden 1967, pp.14-18)

Further Reading

Everything of central importance by Oakeshott has been dealt with or mentioned somewhere above. There is a select bibliography to 1966 in Greenleaf; another, to 1990, in Franco; a full bibliography to 1968, also by Greenleaf, in King and Parekh; and a bibliography 1968-1976, by Auspitz (all references below). The only biography of Oakeshott to date, sketchy as it is, is contained in Chapter 1 of the present work.

The reader anxious to acquaint himself with Oakeshott is advised to read his works in the following order, preferably before consulting any commentaries: R, E, V, C, H (see Textual References above). Oakeshott is generally reckoned to be an elusive writer, and, despite his latter-day efforts at absolute precision, has suffered more than most from misunderstanding or misrepresentation. Some of that has been innocent or insufficiently attentive to detail, while some has almost certainly been wilful or ideologically-motivated. The following seem to me among the more useful, interesting, or historically significant commentaries:

Greenleaf, W.H.: *Oakeshott's Philosophical Politics*, London, 1966. Sympathetic introduction to early and middle-period Oakeshott.

Franco, Paul: *The Political Philosophy of Michael Oakeshott*, New Haven and London, 1990. First single-handed exposition of Oakeshott's total political *oeuvre* (no aesthetics). Thorough, detailed, painstaking, but critically rather bland. Addressed to professional political scientists.

King, Preston, and Parekh, B.C., eds.: *Politics and Experience: Essays Presented to Michael Oakeshott*, Cambridge, 1968. Oakeshott's retirement *Festschrift*. Few essays deal with Oakeshott directly, most with themes suggested by his work. Overall tone grudging, though there are good things.

Auspitz, J.L., and others: 'A Symposium on Michael Oakeshott', *Political Theory*, Vol. 4, no. 3 (August 1976). Apart from Auspitz's first-rate, enthusiastic survey of Oakeshott up to 1976, essentially a collective review of *On Human Conduct*. The other contributors respond with puzzlement, or anger, or both. Includes Oakeshott's reply.

Postan, M.M.: 'Revulsion from Thought', *Cambridge Journal*, Vol. 1 (1947-8), 395-408. Well-meant socialist reply to 'Rationalism in Politics' by Oakeshott's co-editor. Title indicates burden of the charge.

Falck, Colin: 'Romanticism in Politics', *New Left Review*, Jan.-Feb. 1963. Serious, even sympathetic, left-wing critique of Rationalism in Politics.

Crick, Bernard: 'The World of Michael Oakeshott', *Encounter*, June 1963 (reprinted in Crick's *Political Theory and Practice,* London, 1973). Oakeshott the 'Tory dandy' (alternatively, 'Tory anarchist'). Marred by a tedious, self-centred facetiousness that has since become this author's trademark.

Shklar, Judith: review of *On Human Conduct*, *Times Literary Supplement*, 12th September, 1975. Very intelligent, and (though highly appreciative) contains some pertinent criticisms.

Raphael, D.D.: 'On Oakeshott', *Political Quarterly*, October 1975. Prefers Kelsen on authority. Thinks the state's need for self-preservation destroys Oakeshott's distinction between the 'civil' and 'enterprise' states.

Liddington, John: 'Oakeshott: Freedom in a Modern European State', in Gray, J. and Pelczynski, Z., eds., *Conceptions of Liberty in Political Philosophy*, London 1984. Raises tricky questions about 'freedom' in *On Human Conduct*.

Grant, R.A.D.: 'Oakeshott', in *Conservative Thinkers,* ed. R. Scruton, London 1988. Wide-ranging, impressionistic, and wrong, especially about *On Human Conduct*. However, contains things (e.g. on Oakeshott's literary qualities) excluded from the present work on grounds of space, but noted nowhere else.

Gray, John: 'Michael Oakeshott and the Political Economy of Freedom', *The World and I,* September 1988. Highly suggestive, and the best up-to-date short survey. An extended, and academically far more specialist, version constitutes Ch.11 of Gray's *Liberalisms,* London 1989.

The interested reader may also care, for the purposes of comparison, to consult the following authors, referred to in the text but without bibliographical details:

Hayek, F.A.: *The Road to Serfdom* (1944), London, 1962
The Counter-Revolution of Science, Chicago, 1952
The Constitution of Liberty (1960), London, 1963
Law, Legislation and Liberty (1973-9), London, 1982

Polanyi, Michael: *The Logic of Liberty,* Chicago, 1951
Personal Knowledge (1958), London, 1983

Popper, Karl R.: *The Open Society and its Enemies* (1945), London, 1972
The Poverty of Historicism (1956), London, 1972

Ryle, Gilbert: *The Concept of Mind* (1949), Harmondsworth, 1978

Index of Names

Aristotle, 7, 53, 65, 75, 77, 80, 85, 91, 101, 107, 109
Asquith, H.H., 16
Astor, Hon. Michael, 17
Auden, W.H., 20f

Bacon, Sir Francis, 53, 92
Barthes, Roland, 109
Benn, Anthony Wedgwood, 94
Bentham, Jeremy, 8, 14
Bergson, Henri, 35, 38
Bodin, Jean, 70
Bradley, F.H., 13, 29f, 31, 32, 38, 39
Braudel, F., 104
Burckhardt, Jakob, 13, 47, 92
Burke, Edmund, 7, 34, 35, 49, 85-6, 114
Burton, Robert, 100
Butler, Joseph, 80

Carlyle, Thomas, 34, 48, 100
Carr, E.H., 18, 102, 104
Chopin, Frédéric, 108
Coleridge, S.T., 87
Collingwood, R.G., 13, 29, 30, 31, 37, 38, 74, 99

Dante, Alighieri, 108
Darwin, Charles, 40
Derrida, Jacques, 109
Descartes, René, 25, 27, 35, 53, 57
Devlin, Patrick, Lord, 63
Dickens, Charles, 72
Dilthey, Wilhelm, 33, 34, 35, 42, 73, 108
Dostoevsky, Fyodor, 94

Elgar, Sir Edward, 15
Eliot, T.S., 7, 15, 60, 67-8
Epicurus, 63
Evans-Pritchard, E.E., 112

Faulty, Basil, 40
Fitzgerald, Scott, 17
Franco, Paul, 5
Freud, Sigmund, 25, 31, 56, 111
Friedman, Milton, 7, 96
Fromm, Erich, 56

Galbraith, J.K., 7
Gierke, Otto, 90
Godwin, William, 51
Goethe, W. von, 47, 118
Goldmann, Lucien, 102
Grant, Rev. Cecil, 12
Gray, John, 5, 60, 112
Green, T.H., 19, 92
Griffith, G.T., 151
Grote, John, 34, 111

Hardy, Thomas, 108
Hayek, F.A. von, 7, 53, 60, 113f
Hebbel, Christian Friedrich, 33
Hegel, G.W.F., 7, 12, 19, 27-9, 31f, 38, 55, 60, 74f, 79, 83, 93, 117f
Heidegger, Martin, 13, 27, 35
Hemingway, Ernest, 17
Hitler, Adolf, 54
Hobbes, Thomas, 7, 8, 14, 16, 19, 22, 35, 40, 46, 56, 63, 70, 75, 83

Hölderlin, Friedrich, 13
Huizinga, J.H., 66
Hume, David, 7, 35, 77, 83
Husserl, Edmund, 34

Ingres, J.A.D., 108

James, William, 34
Joseph, Sir Keith, 21

Kant, Immanuel, 12, 32, 33, 42, 73, 75, 76, 105, 115
Kelsen, Hans, 84
Kemp, Sandra, 5
Keynes, J.M., Lord, 52
Kierkegaard, S., 57
Knox, T.M., 14, 39

Laski, Harold, 7, 18, 62
Laswell, H.D., 115
Lawrence, D.H., 13, 33
Leavis, F.R., 14
Le Corburier, 52
Leibniz, Gottfried, 25, 39, 40
Lessnof, Michael, 5
Lloyd George, David, 16
Locke, John, 97, 115
Lotze, Hermann, 34
Lysenko, T., 54

MacPherson, C.B., 92
McTaggart, J.M.E., 13, 32
Maitland, F.W., 90, 104
Marsilius of Padua, 63
Marx, Karl, 25, 75, 111, 116
Mill, J.S., 12, 19, 64, 86, 87, 95, 96-7
Montagne, M. de, 12, 47

Montesquieu, Charles-Louis de Secondat, Baron de, 51
Montessori, Maria, 12
Moore, Marianne, 108
Mure, G.R.G., 14

Nabokov, Vladimir, 107
Newman, J.H., Cardinal, 48
Nietzsche, F.W., 13, 75, 94
Nozick, Robert, 8, 114f

O'Hear, Anthony, 5

Pascal, Blaise, 53
Plato, 25, 71f
Polanyi, Michael, 48, 113
Popper, Sir Karl, 58, 113

Rainborough, Colonel, 93
Raphael, D.D., 84
Rawls, John, 8, 114f
Reich, Wilhelm, 56
Rilke, R.M., 111, 112
Roosevelt, F.D., 93
Rorty, Richard, 111
Rousseau, J.J., 32
Ruskin, John, 34
Ryle, Gilbert, 14, 35, 40, 47, 54

Sartre, Jean-Paul, 30
Scheler, Max, 94
Schier, Flint, 5-6
Schoeck, Helmut, 94
Scruton, Roger, 5, 111
Shakespeare, William, 107-8
Shaw, G.B., 11
Shelley, P.B., 51
Smith, Adam, 114

Sobran, Joseph, 5
Spinoza, Benedict, 25, 28, 29, 38, 45
Stebbing, L. Susan, 14
Stephen, Sir James Fitzjames, 63
Strauss, Leo, 115, 116

Theophrastus, 50
Tocqueville, Alexis de, 104
Tolstoy, Leo, 103
Tönnies, Ferdinand, 79, 88-9
Tooke, Horne, 12
Toynbee, Arnold, 115

Valéry, Paul, 66
Vigny, Alfred de, 16
Voegelin, Eric, 115f

Weber, Max, 108
Webb, Sidney and Beatrice, 11f
Wells, H.G., 51
Williams, Raymond, 18
Wilson, Woodrow, 62
Winch, Peter, 112-3
Wittgenstein, L, 14, 35, 49, 111, 112
Woolf, Virginia, 106
Worsthorne, Peregrine, 5, 16

Subject Index

Absolute idealism, 27f, 33, 35, 38
aestheticism, 106f, 109
aesthetics, 38, 76, 105-9
alienation, 93-4
Annales school, 104
art, 38, 47, 65f, 104-9

Bauhaus, 52
bloomers, 52

Cambridge Journal, 17f, 20
capitalism, 92
Cartesianism, 33, 35
categorical imperative, 32
Charter 77, 90
Chicago School economics, 21
church, 60, 88-9
'civil association', 21, 80-83, 87, 88-9, 94
civility, 70, 81f, 84-6, 94f
class feelings, 23-4
collectivism, 7, 16f
communism, 20, 60f
conservatism, 7, 20, 60-64, 116
constitution, 57, 84, 86-7
'contingency', 78-9
conversation, 20, 43, 65-70, 73, 79, 105
culture, 84-6

democracy, 16, 55, 59, 87
dirigisme, 91f

economics, 73-4, 103
Education Acts, 51
empiricism, 26f
Englishness, 15
Enlightenment, 51
'enterprise association', 21, 22, 79-80, 83, 91f, 95
equality, 59

existentialism, 77
Experience, 38, 39f, 42, 46, 66f

Fabianism, 11f
freedom, 59, 93, 95-7, 117
friendship, 88f, 94f, 106-7

geistige Welt, see *Lebenswelt*
General Will, 32
government, 62f

history, 38, 41, 46f, 54, 66, 99-104, 105
horse-racing, 15
human world, 33f

Idealism, 5, 13f, 25f, 30f, 37f, 49, 99f, 111
ideoelogy, 8, 19, 54-6, 76, 112
individualism, 32-3, 55-6, 57, 92f, 113
irrationalism, 35
instrumental thinking, 52f
intelligence, 72-3

knickers, 52
knowing how, 47
knowledge, 47-9

law, 62f, 81-4, 89, 91, 95
Lebenswelt, 34, 37, 42-3, 66, 68, 84, 112
liberalism, 7, 62-3, 86
Logical Positivism, 14, 28
love, 47, 106-7

Marxism, 7, 58, 73, 92, 100, 112, 116

masses, 93-4
modernism, 60f, 94
'modes', Oakeshott's theory, 30, 37-49, 65-70, 71, 73, 99f
'modes', Spinoza's theory, 28, 29
monads, 39
monarchy, 60
morality, 55-6, 69f, 75-8, 81, 84f, 94f, 106-7

nationalism, 85
National Socialism, 13, 35
nation state, 85
Nouvelle Critique, 109

philosophe, 71
philosophy, 30, 39f, 114f
poetry, 104-7
political philosophy, 7
politics, 15, 31f, 51f, 59f, 86-7
poverty, 93-4
practice, 38, 45-9, 55, 58f, 67, 78, 103, 104f, 116f
pragmatism, 34
procedures, 72f
psychoanalysis, 30f, 73
Putney Debates, 93

Rationalism, 18f, 25f, 50-58, 69, 71, 79, 85, 87, 96, 108, 111, 112, 115
rationality, 19, 49, 53f, 69, 114f
religion, 30, 38, 56, 103, 106
Renaissance, 47, 56f, 92
Rights of Man, 51, 59
Roman Catholicism, 16
romanticism, 13, 34

science, 30, 33, 38, 41, 46f, 54,
  55, 66, 105, 113
scientism, 53
self-disclosure, 74f, 79-80
self-enactment, 74f, 96
socialism, 18f, 62f
societas, 88-90
state, 90-95
Stoics, 32
substance, 28, 38

totalitarianism, 15, 61, 91, 113
tradition, 49f, 57-64, 101
truth, 28, 38, 42, 66-67, 71, 99

unconscious, 30f
underwear, 52
universitas, 88-90, 91, 92
universities, 69, 71
utility, 83

Verstehen, 34, 108
virtue, 76-8, 82

Wandervögel, 13
war, experience of, 16f
will, 45-9, 96